MAP OF NORTH AMERICA

Open this fold-out map to see major flight
paths, to chart your route, and to note sights
of interest that you might spot along the way.

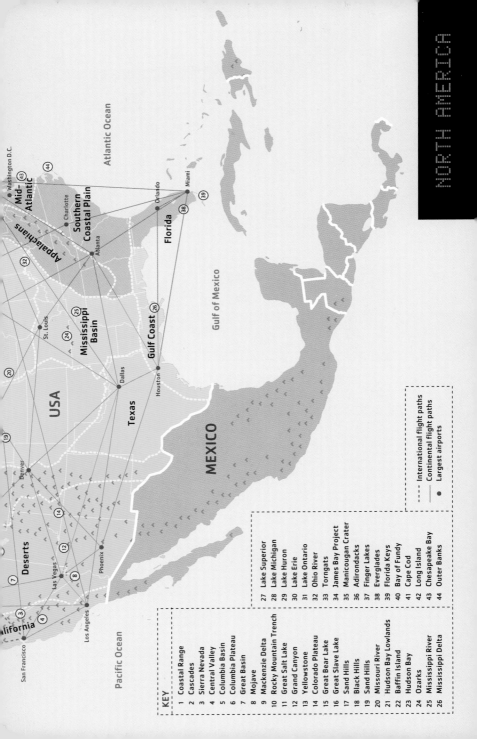

NORTH AMERICA

Pacific Ocean

Atlantic Ocean

Gulf of Mexico

USA

MEXICO

California

Deserts

Texas

Mississippi Basin

Gulf Coast

Florida

Appalachians

Southern Coastal Plain

Mid-Atlantic

San Francisco
Los Angeles
Las Vegas
Phoenix
Denver
Dallas
Houston
St. Louis
Atlanta
Charlotte
Orlando
Miami
Washington D.C.

⑦ ③ ④ ⑫ ⑧ ⑭ ⑲ ⑳ ㉔ ㉕ ㉖ ㉜ ㊳ ㊴ ㊳ ㊹

KEY

1 Coastal Range
2 Cascades
3 Sierra Nevada
4 Central Valley
5 Columbia Basin
6 Columbia Plateau
7 Great Basin
8 Mojave
9 Mackenzie Delta
10 Rocky Mountain Trench
11 Great Salt Lake
12 Grand Canyon
13 Yellowstone
14 Colorado Plateau
15 Great Bear Lake
16 Great Slave Lake
17 Sand Hills
18 Black Hills
19 Sand Hills
20 Missouri River
21 Hudson Bay Lowlands
22 Baffin Island
23 Hudson Bay
24 Ozarks
25 Mississippi River
26 Mississippi Delta

27 Lake Superior
28 Lake Michigan
29 Lake Huron
30 Lake Erie
31 Lake Ontario
32 Ohio River
33 Torngats
34 James Bay Project
35 Manicougan Crater
36 Adirondacks
37 Finger Lakes
38 Everglades
39 Florida Keys
40 Bay of Fundy
41 Cape Cod
42 Long Island
43 Chesapeake Bay
44 Outer Banks

- - - International flight paths
——— Continental flight paths
● Largest airports

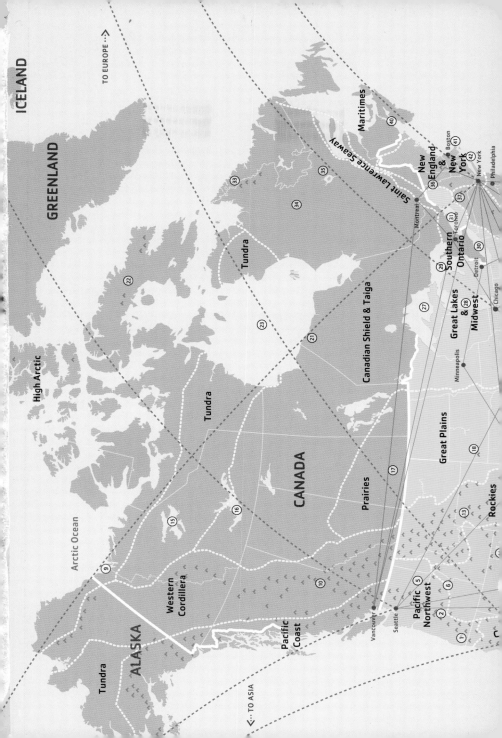

WINDOW SEAT

READING THE LANDSCAPE FROM

WINDOW SEAT

THE AIR

GREGORY DICUM

CHRONICLE BOOKS
SAN FRANCISCO

Copyright © 2003 CNES / Courtesy SPOT Image
Corporation: 33, 114, 115

Copyright © 2003 GlobeXplorer / Airphoto USA:
37, 52, 62, 65, 70, 87, 102

Copyright © 2003 GlobeXplorer / DigitalGlobe:
15, 46, 63, 69, 77, 78, 79, 80, 83, 92, 93, 97,
98, 100, 101, 104, 106, 107, 108, 110, 117 top
and bottom, 119, 120, 121, 122

Copyright © Produced under licence from Her
Majesty the Queen in Right of Canada, with
permission of Natural Resources Canada: 26–27,
128, 130, 131, 133, 134, 136, 138, 139, 141,
143, 144, 145, 147, 149, 150, 153

Provided by USGS: 22–23, 24–25, 34, 35, 36,
40, 41, 45, 49, 50, 51, 54, 55, 56, 57, 73, 74,
84, 85, 86, 88, 102, 118

Library of Congress Cataloging-in-Publication
Data:
    Dicum, Gregory. Window seat : reading the
    landscape from the air/ by Gregory Dicum.
        p.   cm.
    ISBN 0-8118-4086-7
    1. North America—Description and
    travel. 2. Landscape—North America.
    3. North America—Aerial photographs.
    4. Landscape—North America—Aerial
    photographs. I. Title.
    E41.D53 2004
    917'.0022'2—dc21   2003007908

Manufactured in China
Designed by Vivien Sung

Distributed in Canada by Raincoast Books
9050 Shaughnessy Street
Vancouver, British Columbia V6P 6E5

10 9 8 7 6 5 4 3 2 1

Chronicle Books LLC
85 Second Street
San Francisco, California 94105
www.chroniclebooks.com

The joy of surveying a topic as broad as an entire continent was made even greater by the many people who lent me their expertise, advice, and enthusiasm along the way.

Many of the images and much of the information in this book were provided by various branches of the governments of the United States and Canada. All the government personnel I spoke with were a credit to their respective agencies, and unfailingly offered me substantial and timely assistance. In particular, Lynn Charron and David Lemieux at Natural Resources Canada, John Hutchinson and Mitch Adelson at the U.S. Geographical Survey, and Gene Donaldson and Jim Grant at the U.S. Federal Aviation Administration deserve special thanks.

ACKNOWLEDGMENTS

My education stood me in good stead and I am indebted in particular to the Yale School of Forestry and Environmental Studies, where I first learned the art of aerial-photo interpretation. In addition, the various friendly academics from around the continent I spoke with throughout the process of writing this book have left their marks in its pages.

The people who facilitated my searches through the extensive photo libraries of the private sector include Carole Black at SPOT Image, Dave Ruiz at HJW Geospatial, Chuck Herring at Digital Globe, and Kirsten Kemner at GlobeXplorer.

For alleviating various headaches along the way I am grateful to David Stevenson and Paul Yoon at Progrexion and to Nancy Mulvany at the National Writers Union.

The people at Chronicle Books have been a joy to work with, in particular Jodi Davis, whose unwavering editorial hand has made this book such a great read, and Vivien Sung, whose design work has made it a visual feast.

Nina Luttinger, who didn't just put up with our office clutter but loved to have the room littered with maps and photographs, and whose encouragement was indispensable, deserves huge thanks.

Finally, thanks to all the seatmates, cabin crews, and pilots who have answered my questions over the years.

CONTENTS

INTRODUCTION

Taking a commercial passenger flight is one of the unheralded joys of life in the modern world. The food might be utilitarian, the seat cramped, and your neighbor annoying, but the sheer pleasure of contemplating our planet from 35,000 feet (about 6.5 mi., or 10.7 km) in the air is worth any price. A century ago, nobody on Earth could have hoped to see this view, and yet it's yours—free—with every flight you take.

This book is not just for those of us who insist on getting the window seat every time—we who rearrange our travel schedules to guarantee daytime flights, and who look forward to an extra leg or an unplanned detour as an opportunity to examine some new territory. This book is for anyone who has glanced out the window and wondered what that strange pattern on the ground is, or why that huge building is in the middle of nowhere. This book is for the planetary explorer disguised in the ho-hum garb of the modern airline passenger.

Window Seat crams a lot of territory between its covers: Canada and the United States together comprise almost 8 million square miles (about 20 million sq. km), or one-twentieth of the world's land area. Hundreds of possible routes await you, so *Window Seat* can be read in many ways. You can check the map of major routes in the front of the book to figure out what parts of the continent you will pass over on your flight, then follow along as your flight progresses. Or browse the book to learn more generally about what you'll be seeing along the way. Specific elements that appear frequently—in particular, human-created features like interstates and suburbs—are dealt with in detail once and then cross-referenced elsewhere.

Of course, if you're already in the air, your best starting point is to skip straight to the sights you see outside your window. Come back to this introduction later, but don't waste valuable flight time here—who knows what you might be missing!

In the United States, 30,000 airline flights depart each day, carrying 600 million passengers a year on 662 jetways (high-altitude air routes). Because so many trips are possible, this book does not focus only on specific sights. While features of note like the Mississippi River, the Grand Canyon, and Yosemite National Park are covered, more emphasis is given to the general trends you will see on any flight through particular regions, rather than on specifics that depend on more than a little luck to spot.

If you are inclined to undertake more advanced window gazing, a road map is a very handy addition to your carry-on bag. With this resource, you can keep detailed track of your route and identify specific towns and various geographical features. You can also find additional information online at www.windowseat.info.

The aim of *Window Seat* is to help you learn to "read" the landscape below you. My hope is that for those of you who already spend your flights with your noses pressed against the window, this slim volume will further enrich the joy and wonder of gazing down from that exalted perch. For the rest of you, I hope that this book will transform your flying hours into a sublime opportunity to understand our world as never before. ~ *Gregory Dicum*

READING THE LANDSCAPE FROM THE AIR

When, as a small child, you opened a book for the first time, the writing on the pages seemed incomprehensible. But as you acquired just a little knowledge, the letters resolved themselves into words, and the words into meanings. The same goes for reading the landscape. If you know what to look for, gazing out an airplane window is like reading an ever-unfolding scroll on which is written the life-size story of the continent.

From 35,000 feet (10.7 km) in the air, the tiny details fall away. At this altitude, you can't see a particular rock or tree or street—you can see only rock and forest and roads in general. The details are fascinating in their own right, but they distract us from the larger vistas they are a part of. From outside the ordinary human scale, we can see things not normally visible to us.

This vantage point takes a little getting used to. Because people don't ordinarily view the world from this height, we need to learn a new visual vocabulary that will help us make sense of it all. Just as an individual rock, tree, or street can tell a lot about itself, including its history and the history of its place, a whole landscape of rock, forests, and roads contains volumes of information about the area and about the forces acting on it. You just need to learn the alphabet to be able to read the book spread out before you.

If you gaze out your plane window long enough, no matter what kind of landscape is below you, you'll soon spot categories of features. You'll notice mountains, rivers, forests, and towns, and you'll see that each one has distinctive characteristics. These categories of features, which geographers call layers, can be thought of as transparent maps laid down on top of one another to create the whole landscape.

The layers most useful in making sense of what you see out your window are, from the bottom up, rock, water, plants, and people. Each of them, younger and more ephemeral than the last, is dependent on the patterns of the previous layer for many of its features.

Imagine a mountain, tall and solid, and made of pure rock. This is the first layer. Because it reaches so high, the mountain collects rainfall, and streams flow from its slopes into a lake below. This is the second layer. Where there is plenty of water, a forest grows. This is the third layer. Because the forest supplies wood and water is abundant, people build a town on the lake's edge. This is the fourth layer.

You can see that the characteristics of each layer inform those of subsequent layers. But there is also feedback: Streams can carve gorges into the mountainside. The growth of the forest can fill in the lake. People can clear the forest. The landscape you see from your window is a momentary snapshot of constantly changing features acting on each other. But they do so in predictable ways, and if you know a little bit about how the layers influence one another, you can read this snapshot and figure out what has been going on here over not just the past few years but also the past few thousand or even few million years.

So, first, you must be able to identify the layers. This is pretty simple; you've been doing it all your life. You can already tell mountains from forests, for example, so it's just a short leap to be able to identify these broad categories:

Rock

Geology is rock in all its forms, which includes features like sand and mud. The underlying rock, the oldest element of a landscape, often dates back hundreds of millions of years. Though some of its elements may derive from once-living material, this rock is the result of physical and chemical processes like volcanic activity and weathering.

Water

Water is easy to spot—it's shiny and often appears blue. When it's flowing in rivers, it forms long, often sinuous strands across a landscape. And don't forget, it can be frozen, too: snow and ice are just water in a different form.

Plants

If it's green, it's probably plants. The green chlorophyll plants use to capture energy from the Sun is the most readily visible evidence of life on Earth. However, not all biological elements are green, at least not all the time: Watch for earth tones like reds, yellows, and browns as well. In general, look for tufted shapes, green and dun colors, and irregular patterns that parallel geological or hydrological features.

People

Generally, if you see straight lines or right angles, people are responsible for them. The same goes for perfect geometrical shapes like circles or squares. People also produce nearly all ground lights.

You'll quickly learn to tell these landscape layers apart, and you'll soon see that many elements occur in predictable combinations: Water always flows downhill, for example, and smaller rivers flow into bigger ones. You'll also notice that water attracts people—towns and all sorts of industrial facilities are usually found near a water supply.

Once you get a feel for these kinds of relationships and can make sense of what you're looking at, you'll be reading the landscape fluently. The view from the window seat will never be the same again.

The images in this book were taken by satellites orbiting many times higher than any commercial flight (so far). As a result, they look a little different from the views you'll see out your window, but they are the best general resource for picturing our planet. The advent of satellites has changed the way we visualize the world and our place in it.

Everything you will see out your airplane window has been documented by thousands of satellite images. You can find a satellite image of nearly any place on Earth online if you know where to look. You might try starting with www.windowseat.info.

On the following pages, you'll begin to get a sense of why this imagery has had such a profound impact on our sense of place in the world. These exquisite vistas are like reports back from an exotic planet, but one that we can visit. You can take a cruise up the deep fjords of the British Columbia coast, drive around and around in Austin, climb a pingo by the Arctic Ocean, hike to the bottom of the Grand Canyon, trudge across the Arctic barrens, or breathe the cold, fresh air blowing off a Baffin Island glacier.

This dynamic and relentlessly beautiful Earth is our home, and today we can appreciate it as never before. And satellite imagery is just the beginning; commercial jet travel gives everyone a chance to be a planetary observer.

On a long flight you might see any of the varied faces of our continent: steep mountains outside Aspen, Colorado (facing page), suburban sprawl around Langley, Virginia (pages 17–18), urban density in New York City (pages 18–19), rugged coastline off Boston (pages 20–21), a dynamic starburst of roads in San Antonio, Texas (pages 22–23), bucolic farmland next to Chesapeake Bay (pages 24–25), or the glacial wilderness of Baffin Island (pages 26–27).

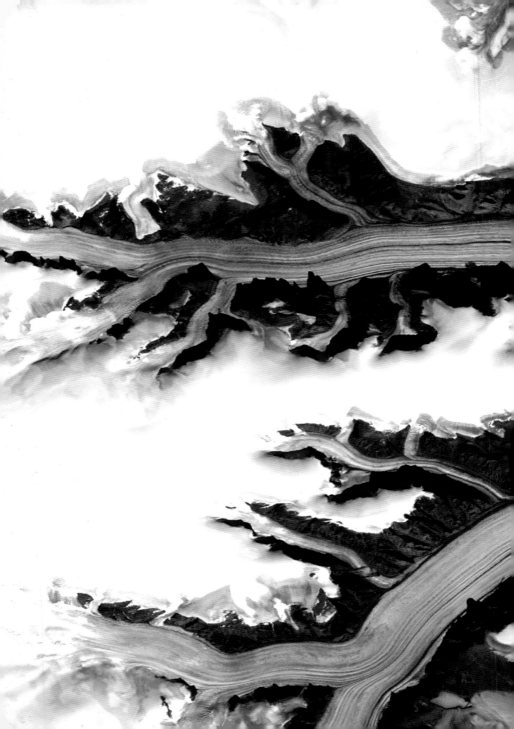

THE EASTERN UNI
S THE EASTERN UN
ATES THE EASTERN
STATES THE EASTER

ED STATES THE EA

TED STATES THE

UNITED STATES T

M UNITED STATES T

Hudson Bay

CANADA

New
England
&
New
York   • Boston

USA   • New York

                              • Philadelphia

              Washington D.C.
                            • Mid-
                              Atlantic

Appalachians

                    • Charlotte

              Atlanta • Southern
                        Coastal Plain   Atlantic Ocean

                                    • Orlando

                              Florida
                                    • Miami

Gulf of Mexico

THE EASTERN UNITED STATES

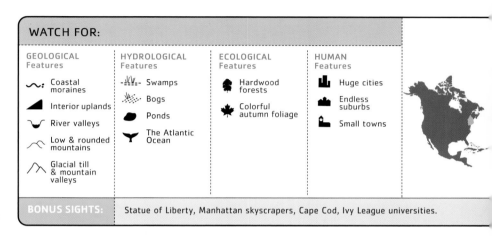

WATCH FOR:

GEOLOGICAL Features	HYDROLOGICAL Features	ECOLOGICAL Features	HUMAN Features
Coastal moraines	Swamps	Hardwood forests	Huge cities
Interior uplands	Bogs	Colorful autumn foliage	Endless suburbs
River valleys	Ponds		Small towns
Low & rounded mountains	The Atlantic Ocean		
Glacial till & mountain valleys			

BONUS SIGHTS: Statue of Liberty, Manhattan skyscrapers, Cape Cod, Ivy League universities.

Beneath its babbling brooks and grassy sand dunes, under the sugar bushes and picturesquely stacked lobster pots, New England is a hard land of rocky mountains and cold shores. It extends inland from the northern Atlantic coast of the United States all the way to the Hudson River Valley in New York. It's pretty dazzling to contemplate the part of the country first colonized by Europeans almost four hundred years ago from the comfort of your jet aircraft—a contraption beyond the wildest dreams of those who first called this place New England.

The basic structure of this region, particularly the rocky uplands, arose from a tectonic collision of African continental material with the North American Plate more than half a billion years ago. The same landmass gave rise, perhaps surprisingly but aptly, to both England and New England (see page 32 for more information about plate tectonics). The collision pushed up the Appalachian Mountains (see page 44 for more information about the Appalachians) of which the mountains of New England are a part, and attached the Boston Basin, an ancient chunk of rock, to North America. As you fly over the Boston area, watch for its undulating form and the occasional outcroppings of gray rock.

The Hudson River Valley marks the rift between these two pieces of the Earth's crust. If you're flying in or out of New York City, see if

PLATE TECTONICS

Like a jelly donut, our planet has a gooey center—a molten metal core and a liquid-rock mantle. Floating on top of this mantle are tectonic plates —enormous sheets of solid rock that form Earth's crust. In areas where the crust is very thick, a continental plate juts skyward and forms dry land; thinner oceanic crust is found deep beneath the ocean.

Currents in the mantle jostle the plates above them, and their collisions create the most spectacular geological features. Mountain ranges form where plates collide or slide over one another, and the most dramatic geological events—including earthquakes and volcanic eruptions— are evidence of this relentless process.

Because the plates move constantly, the positions of the continents and oceans on Earth change over the course of millions of years. Today's world map is just a snapshot of an ongoing rearrangement that can bring regions together or tear them apart and distribute them to opposite sides of the planet.

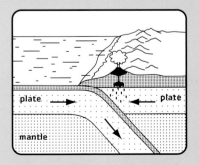

plate →   ← plate

mantle

BOSTON ➤ Much of Boston lies on land created or heavily altered by people. Most of the city to the south and east of down- town (where you see the tall buildings in this image), including Logan International Airport, lies over drained marshes, rivers, and mudflats that have been filled in since the nineteenth century.

you can spot the Palisades, the dramatic cliffs on the west bank of the Hudson River.

If you're above the Boston region, look out to sea, slightly south of the city itself, and you'll see the curving tip of Cape Cod. (You'll also get a good look at the Cape early in flights to Europe from New York City.) A very new feature of the North American coast in geological terms, the Cape formed just ten thousand years ago and is a moraine that marks the end of a great ice sheet that covered New England from the north (see page 66 for more information about moraines and glaciation). The curling northern tip of the Cape with all its highly coveted real estate— including the popular holiday town of Provincetown—is technically a mere spit of sand created by subsequent waves and currents.

Long Island, Martha's Vineyard, Nantucket, and other smaller islands along the southern coast of New England were also formed by this combination of glacial and marine forces. Long Island and Cape Cod are long ridges of sand covered by forest and farms. Nantucket and Martha's Vineyard, the largest islands you'll see here, have a similar look but more rounded shapes. As you fly anywhere between New York City and Boston, notice how different the sandy island and cape terrain appears from the rockier mainland.

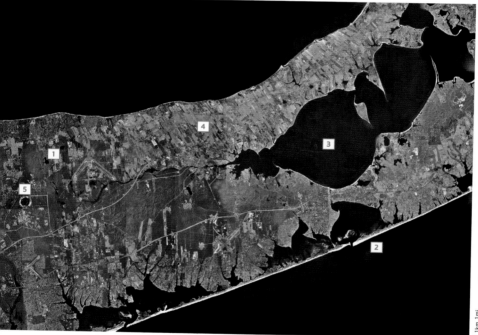

0 1km 1mi

LONG ISLAND ≻ Long Island is a huge terminal moraine, marking the southern limit of the ice sheet that covered the northern part of North America until about ten thousand years ago. The view today includes both glacial features—such as the kettle-pond-strewn ridge at the north of the island **1**—and marine elements, including the barrier beach to the south **2**.

The Hamptons, the towns to the south of the Great Peconic Bay **3**, are resort communities favored by wealthy New Yorkers. The towns to the west are the front edge of suburban sprawl overtaking rich farmland **4**.

The ring of a large particle accelerator **5** marks Brookhaven National Laboratory, established in 1947 to develop peaceful applications for atomic energy.

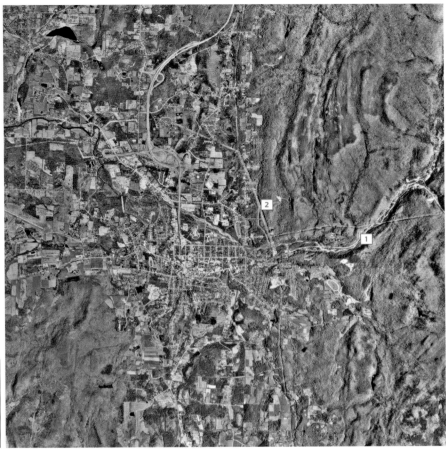

A NEW ENGLAND TOWN ⊱ Settled since 1761, Bennington sits at the western edge of Vermont's Green Mountains—part of the Appalachian mountain system. The traditional New England town layout is a compact grid surrounded by fields that conform to area landforms. Many of these communities feature a village green—a grassy square in the heart of town originally used to provide fodder for horses. Today these picturesque and pleasant greens contribute greatly to the region's unique charm.

Unlike their southern reaches, the Appalachians here were subject to heavy glaciation, which gave the mountains a smoother shape and carved out deep, rounded valleys like the Bolles Brook gorge **1** (compare to the photo on page 45, and see page 66 for more information about glaciation).

Also of note in this image are the long, narrow powerline clearings through the woods and straight over the mountains **2** (see page 87 for more information on the energy system).

A New Forest for New England

New England's rural landscape reflects European—particularly English—preferences, and not just because the two places are both derived from the same archaic landmass. This is the very heartland of British colonization of North America: The Mayflower Pilgrims founded the Massachusetts Bay Colony near what is now Boston in 1620.

By the nineteenth century, nearly all the native forest in New England had been cleared for charcoal making and farming. The land-

THE FINGER LAKES ≻ Here you see Cayuga Lake—one of the eleven Finger Lakes. Carved by glacial action on river valleys over the past two million years, these long, narrow, and very deep lakes are surrounded by classic glacial terrain: Watch for moraines, drumlins, and eskers (see page 66).

Ithaca, New York **1**, the home of Cornell University **2**, is at the southern end of Cayuga Lake **3**.

THE MEGALOPOLIS ➤ North Haven and Hamden, Connecticut, on each side of the Quinnipiac River, blend with other neighboring towns into a sea of suburbs and small satellite cities stretching from Boston to Washington, D.C.

In place of the small town centers that once served as the hubs of distinct communities, the power center **1** next to Interstate 91 now serves the material needs of this conurbation. Hosting the likes of Costco, Target, and Home Depot, these massive developments—often 100 acres (40 ha), with three-quarters of a million square feet of retail space—are both a blessing and a curse: While they provide low-cost material goods to tens of thousands of people in the area, they lack the distinctive social character of the town centers.

The straight lines in the marshland **2** near the power center are channels dug as part of a Works Progress Administration (WPA) project to reduce mosquito habitat during the Great Depression. Adjacent to these marshes is one of the largest tire dumps in the country **3**, holding forty million used tires. Not just ugly, the dump is a fire hazard that leaks toxic effluent and provides habitat for the very mosquitoes the WPA was trying to get rid of.

In spite of this eyesore, life is pleasant here: The streets are lined with large leafy trees, entertainment and jobs are plentiful, wooded hills lie just to the north, and major universities (Yale and the University of Connecticut) are nearby.

scape was a patchwork of small towns and farms separated by fences made of rocks removed from the stony soil. But that gigantic patchwork quilt isn't the landscape you'll see here today: In 1825, with the opening of the Erie Canal, the fertile and much more plow-friendly lands of the

Midwest became available for American settlement, quickly emptying New England of farmers. Flying west across the Hudson River, over upstate New York, you are following the course of this migration; if you keep going, you'll find the missing farms in the Midwest.

With the farmers gone, the New England forest regrew. Thanks to the area's generous and even rainfall and its warm summers, the natural ecosystem here is mixed hardwood forest of oak, maple, hickory, and white pine (in the winter, the pines stand out as dark green dots). These are the woods immortalized by Thoreau, and their resurgence in the past century is one of the brightest spots in America's ecological history.

The blanket of trees below your plane conceals stone fences and abandoned farm roads that mark old field boundaries. In winter, with the leaves gone, you might be able to spot these straight lines carving the forest into squares and rectangles.

If you're flying in the autumn, watch for the celebrated New England fall colors. The golds and reds herald the coming winter as the leaves respond to shorter days and cooler temperatures. This transformation takes place from north to south, from Quebec to Virginia, so if you're flying the same route a week or more later, you should be able to observe changes in this band of color.

In the early spring, watch for the reverse: A crimson mist of billions of tiny red maple blossoms frosts the forest as the sap rises before any new green leaves emerge.

Here and there in this forestland, you can spot ponds and bogs, glittering remnants of depressions in the glacial outwash. Watch for rounded blobs of dark evergreen forest in the middle of the hardwoods: These stands of spruce (in the north) or cedar (in the south) mark the locations of ancient glacial ponds.

While New England's forests have grown, the cities of the area have developed, too. Today, the area from Boston to Washington, D.C., comprises a nearly unbroken megalopolis (a term coined by French geographer Jean Gottmann in 1961 to describe this very region). Forty-four million people—more than one-sixth of the U.S. population—live in this belt, and yet from this height, the hustle is silent and the bustle is invisible. With their halo of wooded suburbs, these massive urban areas constitute one of the most economically and culturally vibrant parts of the world (see page 52 for more information about suburban growth).

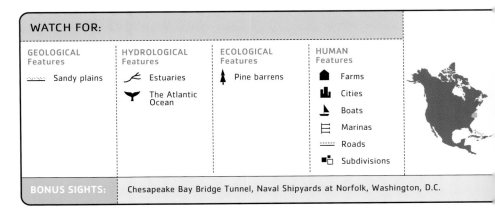

WATCH FOR:

GEOLOGICAL Features	HYDROLOGICAL Features	ECOLOGICAL Features	HUMAN Features
Sandy plains	Estuaries	Pine barrens	Farms
	The Atlantic Ocean		Cities
			Boats
			Marinas
			Roads
			Subdivisions

BONUS SIGHTS: Chesapeake Bay Bridge Tunnel, Naval Shipyards at Norfolk, Washington, D.C.

Chesapeake Bay and Delaware Bay are the defining physical character-istics of the Mid-Atlantic region, which stretches from New Jersey through Virginia. Geologically, this area is part of the coastal plain more prominent farther south, but these massive estuaries (bodies of water contained by land on either side in which seawater and freshwater mix) set it apart. Home to the southern part of the great eastern megalopo-lis, this area includes Philadelphia, Baltimore, and Washington, D.C., as well as many smaller cities (see the photo on page 37).

Thirty-five million years ago, a large asteroid or comet smashed into the planet here, leaving a crater 85 miles (136 km) wide in the con-tinental crust. Today, this enormous depression is buried by sediment under the mouth of Chesapeake Bay, the location of which may have been influenced by this ancient catastrophe.

American history in this region goes right back to the very begin-ning of the European presence. Jamestown, Virginia, established in 1607 at the southern end of Chesapeake Bay, is the oldest extant European settlement in the original thirteen colonies. While you're unlikely to be able to identify this particular town from the air, you'll see that the entire region is covered in a network of irregular roads, small towns, and farms with odd shapes—an indication that this land-scape was laid out long ago.

Estuaries like Chesapeake Bay, the largest in the United States, and Delaware Bay are important fisheries. The mixing of freshwater and saltwater makes estuaries very productive environments, and both human systems and larger, oceanic ecological ones depend on them. However, runoff from land clearing, agriculture, and manufacturing, as well as the effluent of the millions of people living in the area, has led to the extinction of many of the native fish and shellfish.

THE DISTRICT OF COLUMBIA ➤ Designed by eccentric French-born architect and Revolutionary War soldier Pierre L'Enfant, the District of Columbia is unique in the United States. Built on a grid in a 100 square mile (260 sq. km) diamond, the city has many broad, diagonal boulevards that come together to create grand open spaces **1**.

The city center, along the Mall **2**, was designed to house the major institutions of government (including the Capitol **3**) in impressive style.

The District of Columbia is built on land ceded by Maryland and Virginia along the banks of the Potomac River (although the Virginia land was given back later) and does not belong to any state. Once only sparsely settled, the area around the District of Columbia in Virginia and Maryland today houses thousands of government agencies, offices, and facilities, of which the Pentagon **4** is but one example (see page 37 for more information on the megalopolis and page 52 for more information on sprawl).

0 1km 1mi

THE DELMARVA PENINSULA ➤The area around Cambridge, Maryland, on the Delmarva Peninsula, to the east of Chesapeake Bay, exemplifies the intensive agriculture of staples like soy, corn, and wheat around the bay. The branching shape and irregular margins of the bay tell of the flooding of the ancient Susquehanna valley. This sandy coastal area naturally supports pine scrub, much like the pine barrens still found in New Jersey, across the Delaware Bay.

THE INTERSTATE SYSTEM

From your airplane seat, the two parallel lines of blacktop stretching to the horizon might not look like much, but the Dwight D. Eisenhower National System of Interstate and Defense Highways—with 50,000 miles (80,000 km) of roadway—is the largest such network in the world.

Eisenhower had been impressed by Germany's autobahns when he was an invading general in World War II. In 1952, as president, Eisenhower authorized federal funding of the Interstate Highway System, which revolutionized the American landscape by superseding irregular and patchy systems of state and private roads.

Interstates were designed to carry big trucks at high speeds. Opposing traffic is divided on raised roadbeds with wide shoulders so that drivers can concentrate on one thing: getting to their destinations. Innovations like off-ramps and cloverleaf interchanges link roads with little disruption in traffic flow.

Even its numbering system is designed for efficiency: North-south routes are given odd numbers and east-west routes have even numbers. Bypasses, which allow drivers to avoid congested urban areas, are numbered using three digits—the number of the parent road plus a multiple of 100 (I-470, for example, connects with I-70 to form a detour around Kansas City).

True to its military roots, the interstate system has important national-defense features: Reputedly, in the event of war, highways throughout the country can double as airfields, but, most important, these roads are essential for quick deployment of military assets.

With a free and fast public road network, the nation shifted from trains to trucks for much of its haulage. In turn, manufacturing centers moved outside of city cores. Commuting great distances to work became possible, fueling the country's suburbanization and furthering the decline of urban centers.

The interstate system touches the lives of everyone in America, including yours: Chances are you used it on your way to the airport today.

Watch for the Potomac winding lazily through the woodlands, fields, and suburbs of Virginia and Maryland—it forms the border between these two states. As early as the nineteenth century, Washington, D.C., residents, including Abraham Lincoln, fled the city during the summer months because of the stench of sewage in the Potomac River. While the ecological decline of Chesapeake Bay had been noted as early as 1639, it is only in recent decades that local governments have undertaken serious efforts to reverse the damage.

Today, seventeen million people live in the heavily developed Chesapeake Bay region, and, as you fly over it, you'll see farms, subdivisions, urban areas, shipyards, marinas (look for tight arrays of docks with lots of small, light-colored boats), industrial facilities, and tourist developments (watch especially for condominiums or hotels next to golf courses). At the mouth of the bay, where it enters the Atlantic, you might also spot the Chesapeake Bay Bridge-Tunnel, a series of structures 18 miles (29 km) long that connects the tip of the Delmarva Peninsula to the Virginia mainland near Norfolk. Opened to great fanfare in 1964, this roadway alternately rides high above the water and plunges into tunnels deep beneath the waves to allow large ships to cross overhead.

THE APPALACHIANS

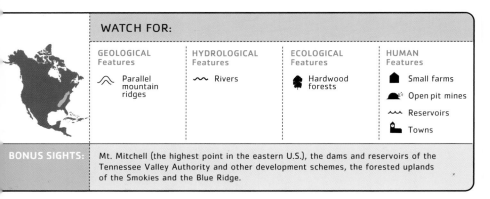

WATCH FOR:

GEOLOGICAL Features	HYDROLOGICAL Features	ECOLOGICAL Features	HUMAN Features
⌒ Parallel mountain ridges	∿ Rivers	🌲 Hardwood forests	🏠 Small farms
			⛏ Open pit mines
			∿∿ Reservoirs
			🏘 Towns

BONUS SIGHTS: Mt. Mitchell (the highest point in the eastern U.S.), the dams and reservoirs of the Tennessee Valley Authority and other development schemes, the forested uplands of the Smokies and the Blue Ridge.

Most geological activity moves so slowly that it is very difficult to detect over the course of a human lifetime (rather the opposite of a plane ride). Nonetheless, it possesses a power so vast as to create the massive physical structures upon which we live our little lives.

Nearly six hundred million years ago, North America and Africa smashed into one another in a slow-motion collision that lasted fifty million years (see page 32 for more information about plate tectonics). In the process, the margins of both continents folded like the edges of two rugs being pushed into one another. These ripples reached as high as today's Himalayas. But over hundreds of millions of years, erosion has worn them down into today's remnant ranges: the Appalachians in North America and North Africa's Atlas Mountains. Today, Mount Mitchell, the highest point in the Appalachians, reaches 6,684 feet (2,037 m) in the Great Smoky Mountains of North Carolina.

As you look down on the Appalachians, you can see the signs of this collision: row after row of northeast-to-southwest ridges. It is no accident that the thirteen original U.S. states are all on the eastern side of these mountains, for this was long a treacherous and impenetrable wilderness that prevented all but the most determined from moving westward.

The Appalachians stretch from the Deep South all the way to the Gaspé Peninsula in Quebec, but the cultural region known as Appalachia usually refers to that part of the range stretching from Mississippi, Alabama, and Georgia through to Pennsylvania and southern New York state.

Always a bit wild, Appalachia served as a refuge for indigenous peoples (Cherokee and others), escaped slaves, minority immigrant communities (some, like the Melungeons of southern Appalachia, of mysterious origin), and whites (especially the Scotch-Irish, who introduced whiskey making to the region) fleeing the law and order of British and later American authorities. Still, development has visited this region, mostly in the form of coal mining, which brought tens of thousands of mainly Eastern European miners to dig up these hills in

0 1km 1mi

APPALACHIA ⤝ Near where Tennessee, Virginia, and North Carolina all come together in the heart of Appalachia, the mountain ridges of the Cherokee National Forest are evidence of an ancient collision of continents. Unlike the Appalachian ranges farther north (see the photo on page 35), these ridges do not show signs of recent glaciation. Rather, the rock here was worn down by wind and rain over the eons. You can see this difference in the drainage patterns, which are more finely dendritic (resembling the structure of a tree's branches). Forest of mixed hardwoods covers the ridges and slopes, with small hay, dairy, and tobacco farms in the bottomlands. This picturesque landscape attracts millions of visitors each year, making tourism by far the biggest industry in the region.

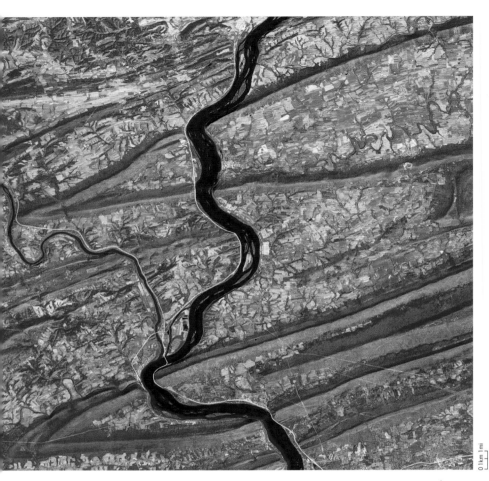

0 1km 1mi

THE SUSQUEHANNA ➤ The Susquehanna River, which breaks through the unmistakable parallel ridges of the Appalachians just outside Harrisburg, Pennsylvania, flows through an important coal region, and was a key resource for the development of the mining and smelting industries here. The fertile valleys between the ridges, long settled and divided into small farms by, among others, Pennsylvania Dutch (including Amish) communities, retain a bucolic old-world feel in spite of their proximity to the megalopolis of the coast.

the nineteenth and early twentieth centuries. Mining is still important here: Watch for open pits and heaps of refuse rock that stand out against the green forests and farms.

The greatest urban center of this region is Pittsburgh. The lucky combination of nearby coal, limestone, and iron ore reserves, plus the waterways of the Mississippi and the Great Lakes, made Pittsburgh the key American steel-making center in the nineteenth century. The hardware for the rapidly developing nation—including the frames of New York and Chicago skyscrapers, the rails of the transcontinental railway, and the cables of great spans like the Brooklyn Bridge—were forged here from Appalachian ore and sweat. Around Pittsburgh, you'll still see huge industrial foundries—gigantic installations with huge, dark pipes, cylindrical blast furnaces, and tall smokestacks.

Today, tourists flock to these mountains to hike, hunt, fish, raft, camp, and tour. If it's summertime, look for the boxy white shapes of RVs on the roads.

THE SOUTHERN COASTAL PLAIN AND THE APPALACHIAN PIEDMONT

WATCH FOR:

GEOLOGICAL Features	HYDROLOGICAL Features	ECOLOGICAL Features	HUMAN Features
Low plains	Rivers	Forestlands	Farms
The Fall Line	Rapids	Salt marshes	Sprawl
Barrier islands	Coastal marshes		
	The Atlantic Ocean		

BONUS SIGHTS: Atlanta's skyscrapers, coastal marshes, Kitty Hawk.

The Southern Coastal Plain comprises all the land north of the Florida Peninsula between the Appalachian Mountains and the Atlantic Ocean from Virginia through Mississippi.

This flat, sandy low-lying area is an exposed part of the North American continental shelf. It has been both underwater and far wider at different times, depending on sea-level fluctuations over millions of years.

The Piedmont consists of the higher ground you see rising to become the foothills of the Appalachians. The long step where the Piedmont meets the Southern Coastal Plain is called the Fall Line, because most of the rivers flowing eastward from the Appalachians have rapids or falls here. You might even be able to spot them: Watch for areas of white water in river courses.

Early European settlers found the Southern Coastal Plain too hot and swampy for comfort, so most of the major cities in this region (including Montgomery, Macon, Augusta, Columbia, Raleigh, and Richmond), and hundreds of smaller communities, are strung along the Fall Line. This more hospitable perch also provided settlers with a ready source of waterpower. As you fly over the region, see if you can spot the transition between the hilly Piedmont and the flat Southern Coastal Plain.

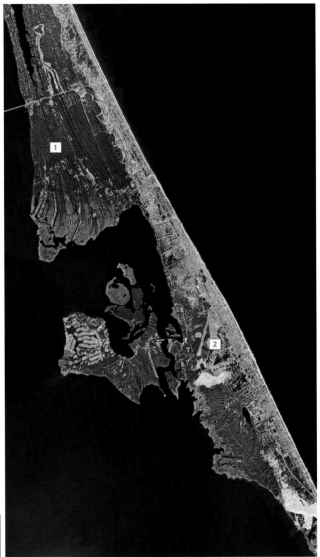

has been a popular resort since 1830.

To the east, or "inside" the Outer Banks, runs the Intracoastal Waterway. This aquatic highway, a combination of canals and natural waterways, extends 3,000 miles (4,800 km) along most of the coast from Boston to Mexico, ensuring safe passage for all manner of boats (see the photo on page 73 for another look).

Pause for a moment as you fly over this region to consider the special meaning it has for you today: it was at Kill Devil Hill **2** that the Wright Brothers achieved powered flight for the first time. That was 1903, little more than a century ago, and the flight lasted just 12 seconds.

NAG'S HEAD, NORTH CAROLINA ➤ The Southern Coastal Plain meets the Atlantic Ocean in a line of sandy bays and barrier islands—exposed sandbars (note the old bars behind the current shore **1**) that provide magnificent recreational opportunities. Nag's Head, in North Carolina's Outer Banks,

the southern coastal plain and the appalachian piedmont

Along with the Mississippi Basin, this region is the heartland of the South. Here, the enormous slave-powered plantations supported the Confederacy, and these lands were drenched with much of the blood spilled in the Civil War.

Atlanta dominates economic and cultural life in the Southern Coastal Plain and the Piedmont. Its new skyscrapers and sprawling suburbs epitomize the New South, an outward-looking, globally integrated economy. A young city, almost brand new when the Civil War broke out, Atlanta is now a trading and transportation hub: As you fly over the region, you'll see that virtually every road and rail line of

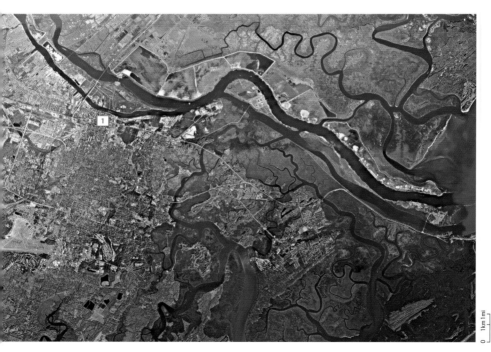

0   1km 1mi

SAVANNAH, GEORGIA ➤ The winding sloughs around Savannah, Georgia, are typical of the salt marshes and swamps—important habitat for birds, fish, and other animals—found along low, flat shores. Sited on a bluff that lifts it out of the coastal swamp and the Savannah River's flood zone, Savannah was the toehold of the thirteenth English colony on the Eastern Seaboard (South Carolina is just to the north, on the other side of the river). Savannah still retains the compact and charming old center **1** dictated by the local geography, as you can see in this image.

THE SOUTHERN FOREST ⊱ The sawmill **1** outside Prosperity, South Carolina (population 1,116) **2** produces plywood and lumber. The mill draws timber from the Southern Coastal Plain and the Appalachian Piedmont. For the most part, the "forests" here are tree plantations that are harvested again and again (see if you can spot the orderly rows of uniform trees). Owned by giant multinationals, local timber companies, and individual small landowners, these tree farms—most of which once grew more familiar crops—make the region the main timber producer in the United States. The irregular shapes of the landholdings arise from the organic patterns of early settlement in the region in the 1830s, as well as post–Civil War attempts at land redistribution.

consequence heads through Atlanta—a bold collection of glass, steel, and concrete rising out of the richly wooded Piedmont. And this tradition continues: Atlanta's Hartsfield International Airport, with one million flights and eighty million passengers a year, has recently become the busiest in the world.

SPRAWL

Suburban sprawl features curvy or squiggly street layouts within large "superblocks" separated by major roads. First applied in Radburn, New Jersey, in 1928, this design was intended to combine the best of urban and rural living. However, it created something altogether new: the American suburb.

Below, suburbs north of Plano, Texas, are part of the contiguous Dallas sprawl. This "warped parallel" layout was in use during the 1960s and 1970s and helps date the development, as do the midsize street trees. More examples of suburban sprawl can be found on pages 56, 63, 70, 77, 85, 117, and 123.

Although the first shopping malls were a Victorian European innovation, it is in the American suburbs that they have been realized to their fullest. The malls **1** in this image are typical, if small. Boxy structures surrounded by expansive parking lots, they contribute to the automotive focus of the suburban landscape. Strip malls, another variant, are linear collections of buildings and parking lots that line major suburban roads.

Since the late twentieth century, the majority of Americans have lived their lives in these specialized zones of land use: housing in one place, shopping in another, and work in yet another, with public space limited to functional structures like roadways or areas where the natural landscape cannot be obliterated, as around Spring Creek **2** at the lower right of this image.

Suburbs of Plano, Texas

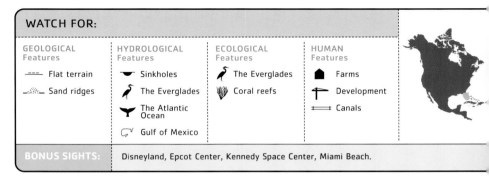

WATCH FOR:

GEOLOGICAL Features	HYDROLOGICAL Features	ECOLOGICAL Features	HUMAN Features
Flat terrain	Sinkholes	The Everglades	Farms
Sand ridges	The Everglades	Coral reefs	Development
	The Atlantic Ocean		Canals
	Gulf of Mexico		

BONUS SIGHTS: Disneyland, Epcot Center, Kennedy Space Center, Miami Beach.

Florida is unmistakable from the air: From up here, it is a flat, visibly wet peninsula surrounded by blue seas. Over the past several hundred million years, a thick deposit of soft limestone composed of corals and other marine life formed here at the bottom of a shallow and warm sea. The resulting rock measures up to 20,000 feet (6,100 m) thick. Such accumulation, still taking place offshore, removes carbon dioxide from the atmosphere, helping regulate Earth's surface temperature—and no doubt laying the foundation for future golf courses.

Like the Southern Coastal Plain, the exposed arm of Florida is part of a much larger feature, the Florida Platform. The peninsula has widened and narrowed as sea levels fluctuated over thousands of years. You'll notice that the seas around Florida, particularly to the west, where the platform extends 100 miles (160 km) from Tampa, are often extremely shallow and appear very light blue (see page 55 for more information about water colors). To the east, the platform extends only a few miles from Miami before dropping 10,000 feet (3,050 m) into the dark blue depths of the Gulf Stream.

Rainwater slowly dissolves and molds limestone, creating karst, a landscape of underground rivers, sinkholes, and lagoons. As you fly over Florida, you will be able to pick out sinkholes—small, round lakes where a cavern has collapsed, exposing the water table. Watch, too, for marshy areas, often filled with tufted green mangrove trees—these are coastal lagoons.

Like the Southern Coastal Plain, the northern part of Florida is covered with Appalachian sand, and you will see sand ridges that were

THE EVERGLADES ≻ South of Lake Okeechobee **1**, the Everglades form an unbroken grassy wetland **2** all the way to the tip of Florida. In the 1940s, about half of the Everglades, which once covered 4 million acres (1.6 million ha), were drained to create fertile and highly productive farmland **3**. But in the absence of the natural system, which renews the soil, this land has been sinking. Worse, nutrient-laden fertilizer runoff threatens the remaining Everglades.

The tiny town of Clewiston **4** is the home of US Sugar, a giant, privately held conglomerate that dominates agriculture in South Florida. On its nearly 200,000 acres (81,000 ha) in this region, the company turns out almost a million tons of sugar each year—one tenth of U.S. consumption.

deposited five million years ago when the area was underwater. Farther south, the Everglades, the only subtropical wet savanna (marshy freshwater grassland) in the United States, is a giant limestone sponge through which a broad river of freshwater flows south to the sea. From the air, it looks like a flat, brownish-green soup with as much exposed water as plant material.

WATER COLORS

Water absorbs long wavelengths of light (which we experience as warm colors like red, orange, and yellow), so the light reflected from the water's depths is mostly of the shorter wavelengths (cool colors like blue).

Shallow areas with clear water and light bottoms—like the Caribbean Sea, where the seabed is composed of white coral sands—reflect light the most brightly. The deeper the water, therefore, the deeper the blue, with the midoceanic depths appearing very dark.

Suspended particles in water also impart color: Runoff from the surrounding land gives many rivers a matching color. (Glacial streams, for example, are often milky with fine silt.) Watch for places were bodies of water containing different-colored particles come together, and you'll be able to see how they mix.

The Florida Keys

Greens are usually due to algae, while plankton, bacteria, and red algae cause the bright reds you sometimes see in salt-evaporation ponds and warm ocean waters.

Ice and snow appear white, as when pack ice accumulates on large bodies of water like the Great Lakes and the Arctic Ocean in jagged white shards separated by raised seams.

THE MAGIC KINGDOM ➤ The various resorts and entertainment complexes of Disney World **1** and Epcot Center **2** to the southwest of Orlando attract nearly 40 million visitors a year, making the area the top tourist destination in the United States. Two-thirds of the people in the area are employed in tourism—part of the world's largest industry, with revenues of half a trillion dollars. Indeed, since 75 percent of all international travel is for the purpose of tourism, there's a very good chance you're participating right now.

The round freshwater lakes **3** that dot this landscape are the result of a combination of karst (limestone riddled with caves and underground channels) and a high water table. Where a cavern's roof collapses to form a sinkhole, the water table is exposed, creating a lake. To the southwest of the complex you can see some remaining orange groves **4**—remnants of the landscape here before Disney arrived in 1971.

This flat, wet, warm, and fertile landscape is ideal for agriculture, and you'll see many kinds of crops here that are rarely grown in the rest of the United States. Sugarcane and rice grow happily in the southern wetlands: Look for shimmering, lined fields of light green or tan

KEY WEST, FLORIDA ➤ The Florida Keys, the southernmost and most tropical part of the continental United States, are old coral reefs exposed by lowered sea levels. Today, live reefs are building up to the south. But the seas may soon cover the Keys again: All around the world, rising sea levels caused by global warming threaten low-lying areas.

As this image shows, shallow waters ring the islands, with bottom details, including bars and channels created by the prevailing currents and tides **1**, clearly visible

from the air (see page 55 for more information on the color of water). Straight channels **2** were cut by people to allow boats into the shallow waters around the Keys. The white smears in the water **3** are the wakes of boats; a pointier, more acute wake indicates faster travel.

Key West, the westernmost key, is a major tourist destination and is almost entirely developed. In the middle, Boca Chica Key hosts a large naval air station **4**. During the Cold War, this base faced off against a Soviet installation in Cuba just 90 miles

(145 km) to the south—if you're flying here, look south and try to spot the island nation. The slender roadway that connects the Keys **5** is the southern terminus of Route 1, which proceeds all the way up the East Coast to Maine.

The dark areas at the edges of the Keys are mangrove forests. Greenish-brown blobs in the water are beds of sea grasses. Both are important habitat for fish and prevent the erosion of beaches and islands, but development and pollution threaten them.

divided into uniform rectangles. You can also see orange trees and other citrus groves farther north as rows of dark green tufted foliage.

Florida, of course, is also famous for its tourist destinations, from Key West in the south through Miami, Disney World, and the Kennedy Space Center farther north. Chances are, that's why you've come here.

TED STATES THE CO

TED STATES THE T

UNITED STATES T

UNITED STATES

CANADA

Great Plains

Minneapolis

**Great Lakes
&
Midwest**

Detroit

Chicago

Denver

USA

St. Louis

**Mississippi
Basin**

Dallas

Texas

Houston

Gulf Coast

Gulf of Mexico

MEXICO

THE CENTRAL UNITED STATES

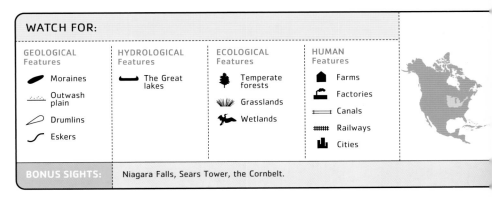

WATCH FOR:

GEOLOGICAL Features	HYDROLOGICAL Features	ECOLOGICAL Features	HUMAN Features
Moraines	The Great lakes	Temperate forests	Farms
Outwash plain		Grasslands	Factories
Drumlins		Wetlands	Canals
Eskers			Railways
			Cities

BONUS SIGHTS: Niagara Falls, Sears Tower, the Cornbelt.

By far the most compelling feature of the Midwest is the Great Lakes. From above, they are featureless blue (or white, when frozen) spaces that mimic the sky itself in their immensity. Formed as little as ten thousand years ago by the most recent Ice Age (see page 66 for more information about glaciation), the Great Lakes are among the youngest major geographical features on the continent. Together they constitute the largest freshwater lake system on Earth, accounting for one-fifth of the world's fresh water. Each of the five lakes, Superior, Michigan, Huron, Erie, and Ontario, is one of the fifteen largest in the world. The largest, Lake Superior, is up to 1,333 feet (406 m) deep and contains enough water to cover the entire continental United States to a depth of 4.25 feet (1.3 m).

From the air, these lakes are unmistakable—they're huge! They cover a total of 94,000 square miles (243,000 sq. km) and contain 6 quadrillion gallons (23 quadrillion liters) of water. In many ways, these "lakes" are seas: In addition to the rich sport and commercial fishery, the pounding surf, the tides, and the complex ecosystems, their very presence is enough to moderate the otherwise harsh weather of the continental interior.

Because of the relatively moderate climate, the Great Lakes are surrounded by extraordinary ecosystems, including dunes, prairies, and lush forests. The marshy wetlands you see along the shores—flat,

500m 0.5mi

THE INDUSTRIAL HEARTLAND ➤ The General Motors (GM) plant in Lansing, Michigan, employed 23,000 workers during its heyday in the 1970s, when it was the largest car-assembly plant in North America.

The auto industry was a source of great pride here. This is reflected in the geography of Lansing itself: The plant is at the heart of the town, just across the Grand River from the Lansing Country Club (the golf course on the left).

GM cars are now in large part made elsewhere, where labor costs and environmental standards are lower, and the Lansing plant was mostly abandoned until 2001, when a new facility was built here. It now takes 1,500 employees—and hundreds of robots—just 24 hours to build a Cadillac from scratch.

uniformly green or brown areas where rivers enter the lakes—provide critical habitat for fish, birds, and large mammals like moose.

On flights crossing this region, particularly between New England and Great Lakes destinations like Detroit and Chicago, as well as points west, including California, you might even be able to see Niagara Falls (see the photo on page 135), which drains Lake Erie into Lake Ontario near Buffalo, New York. From the sky, you'll see the cloud of mist

0 1km 1mi

THE CORN BELT ➤ The rolling glacial outwash terrain outside Columbus, Ohio, is the eastern edge of the Midwest Cornbelt, which extends uninterrupted all the way to the middle of the continent. Corn is the largest crop in the United States, planted on 73 million acres (30 million ha). Sixty percent of corn grown in the United States is used as animal feed, and one-quarter is exported.

As demographics in this region change—fewer people farm and more commute to service jobs—subdivisions (the squiggly new roads appearing on this farmland) spread out from regional centers in uncontrolled sprawl (see page 52 for more information about sprawl).

thrown into the air by the falls' thundering waters. Like the rest of the Great Lakes system (except Lake Michigan), the falls mark the boundary between Canada and the United States.

It's not surprising that more than one-tenth of the U.S. population and one-quarter of Canadians live in the Great Lakes–Saint Lawrence drainage, for the abundant waters and moderate climate make it especially hospitable. Since 1909, the two nations have attempted to maintain a consistent flow of water through the system, whose maintenance is crucial for millions of people. Each day, municipalities remove tens of billions of gallons for everything from irrigation to simple drinking water.

Perhaps inevitably, the once pristine and unique ecology of the Great Lakes has suffered greatly. Pollution from hundreds of industrial installations—one-fifth of U.S. and one-half of Canadian manufacturing takes place here—drains into the lakes. In 1980, after millions of pounds of toxic chemicals were dumped in Love Canal, near Niagara Falls, it became the first site of an industrial incident to be declared a U.S. federal disaster area. Thankfully, this emergency spurred regulatory changes, including a binational effort to clean up the lakes that has begun to show results—the water is getting cleaner, and many fish species are recovering.

Rich glacial till and postglacial windblown silt made the Midwest a natural area for agricultural settlement, and the Great Lakes and the Mississippi River system linked this region to the growing cities east of the Appalachians. This area still grows much of the nation's grains, notably corn. Cornfields appear lushly green in the spring and summer, becoming tawny as they ripen towards the fall. In the winter, look for the sepia tint of stubble on the snowy landscape.

As the Industrial Revolution arrived on American shores from Europe in the late nineteenth century, the Midwest, with its abundant transportation links and raw materials, became one of the most important heavy-manufacturing regions in the world and the backbone of America's global economic power.

As you fly over the region, watch for the remnants of this once-mighty manufacturing sector: huge factories throughout Chicago and Detroit, steel mills around Pittsburgh, and railways everywhere. Railways look like roadways, but they are usually lighter, with the dark ties visible in the center. Unlike roads, railways do not have intersections—they merge into one another instead. Watch for rail yards—places at which the tracks branch into many parallel sets—where trains are loaded and assembled for long journeys.

Chicago, the region's dominant city, pioneered the model of massive centralization that is now a hallmark of the American economy.

1mi

1km

0

CHICAGO ➤ This image of the central part of the city shows the hub of a transportation network that stretches west to the Great Plains by rail and road, south to the Mississippi along the Chicago River, and east by road, rail, and Lake Michigan.

The terrain here is typical of the flat glacial outwash throughout the southern Great Lakes: a sandy shoreline and flat land interspersed with rolling glacial hills. The Chicago River, the canal through the center of town, has been made to breach a moraine along the shore and so connect the two great watersheds of the Mississippi and the Great Lakes.

The stockyards around Chicago—made notorious in 1906 by Upton Sinclair's exposé *The Jungle*—were the final destination for trains from all across the Great Plains. They brought millions of animals here for slaughter, processing, and export to the East Coast and the world. The Chicago stockyards are gone now, buried under city sprawl; the development of refrigeration and even faster transportation prompted these facilities to move into the Great Plains where the cattle are raised (see the photo on page 79).

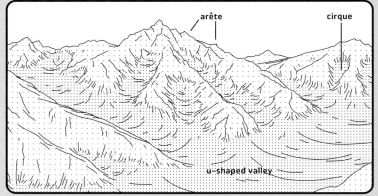

arête   cirque

u-shaped valley

GLACIAL TERRAIN

For most of the past 100,000 years, sheets of ice several miles thick—halfway to the height of your plane—covered all of Canada and much of the United States (particularly the Great Lakes, the Midwest, the Rockies, and New England). The ice began to retreat from the southern reaches of this range about 18,000 years ago, though it remains to this day in parts of the High Arctic.

Glaciers form when snow persists through the summer and builds up. The snow is compacted to ice and takes on liquid characteristics, flowing in (glacially) slow motion across the landscape and carving the land into distinct features.

Mountainous Areas

Mountain ranges accumulate ice caps during periods of cool climate—indeed, most of the remaining glaciers are in mountainous areas. The topography of most ranges has been heavily influenced by this ice.

Cirques are bowl-like valleys surrounded by high, steep walls. A glacier once sat here (and might still—remnants lie in cirques as far south as the Sierra Nevada in California). Arêtes are sharp ridges between cirques (see the photo on page 146 for examples of both arêtes and cirques).

U-shaped valleys are long and broad with high, steep sides. These valleys, often featuring streams running through them, were once the courses of flowing glaciers (see the photo on page 36). Along the coast, these valleys may be flooded to form fjords (see the photo on page 149).

Lowland Areas

The ice caps left plains of outwash—till (sand and gravel) deposited by meltwater—across the entire northeastern sector of North America.

Moraines are high ridges of glacial till pushed up by the front and sides of moving glaciers or deposited at the foot of stationary ones. The size of moraines indicates the scale of the glaciers that created them—some of the largest are hundreds of miles long (see the photo on page 34).

Eskers are sinuous ridges left by rivers that once flowed under ice sheets (see the photo on page 138). Road surfaces are often located at their crests because of their convenient form.

Drumlins, also called whaleback hills, are distinguished by a high, rounded side and a long, tapering side. Across a landscape, groups of drumlins all point in the same direction, parallel to the ancient glacier's motion (see the photo on page 138).

Kettle ponds are round ponds or swamps created by melting chunks of ice left behind as a glacier receded (see the photo on page 34).

Spillways are deep, wide valleys that once carried huge rivers of glacial meltwater. Many now have a much smaller river meandering across the bottom of the outsized valley (see the photo on page 132).

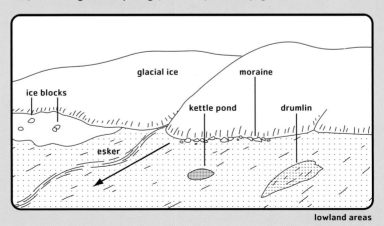

lowland areas

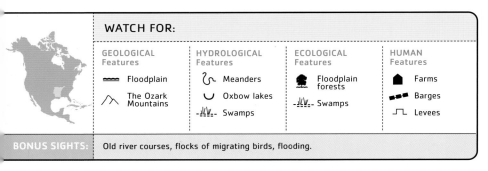

WATCH FOR:

GEOLOGICAL Features	HYDROLOGICAL Features	ECOLOGICAL Features	HUMAN Features
Floodplain	Meanders	Floodplain forests	Farms
The Ozark Mountains	Oxbow lakes	Swamps	Barges
	Swamps		Levees

BONUS SIGHTS: Old river courses, flocks of migrating birds, flooding.

You know you're flying over the Mississippi region when you see the wide, muddy Mississippi river winding through the landscape below. The Mississippi River drains the Rockies, the Great Plains, the Appalachians, the Ozarks, the Midwest, and the lower reaches of the Canadian Shield. The waters from all these regions come together in the Mississippi Embayment, a vast, flat floodplain that stretches 500 miles (800 km) inland to Illinois from the river's delta in the Louisiana waters of the Gulf of Mexico.

Snaking back and forth like a continental intestine, the Mississippi meanders across this plain between the Appalachians to the east and the Ozarks to the west with a sluggishness belying its status as one of the great rivers of the world. Like the Delta farther south, all the flat land you see in this broad valley was deposited over the past sixty million years as the river drained the constantly eroding mountain ranges at its headwaters. Sandy uplands, remnants of a higher floodplain deposited when the river drained the melting continental ice cap during the latest Ice Age, form the shoulders of this plain.

Most of the silt today comes from the west, from the Rockies and the Great Plains. As you fly over the continent, you might be able to spot the difference between the muddy rivers flowing out of the west—the Missouri, for example—and the clearer eastern rivers, like the Ohio, that flow from the older, more heavily eroded Appalachians. These mountains gave up most of their silt eons ago.

With spring rains and mountain meltwaters, the Mississippi often floods large parts of its floodplain, enriching it with fresh deposits of silt and mud. Look for places where the river channel appears to widen

0 1 km 1 mi

THE MISSISSIPPI RIVER ≻ At its confluence with the Arkansas River, the Mississippi River is a riot of oxbows and meanders typical of water flowing across a flat, silty plain. Meanders dig into the bank at the outside of their bends **1** and deposit fresh sand and silt (white treeless areas) on the inside point bars **2**, thus continually renewing the landscape. Oxbow lakes **3** are formed where meanders break through the necks between bends. These lakes slowly fill in and become first cypress swamps, then areas of bottomland hardwood forest.

Along most of its length, the Mississippi's dynamic channel is contained between high levees. These appear from the air as straight lines **4** separating farmland from the native forest and wetlands along the river.

The forest floods annually, so it is unsuitable for agriculture, but the rich fields outside the levees produce cotton, rice, and other crops in abundance. Old river courses are clearly visible under the farmland **5**, showing where the untamed river once flowed freely over the basin and highlighting the forces that the U.S. Army Corps of Engineers is up against here in the largest levee district in the world.

1mi

1km

0

THE ORIGINAL HUB ➤ Memphis International Airport is the headquarters for FedEx and one of four transportation hubs the company maintains around the world. If you fly through here, watch for dozens of white, purple, and orange planes. Although it carries no passengers, FedEx is the ninth-largest airline in the world, and as a result, this is the largest cargo airport.

Since the 1980s, most United States airlines have adopted the hub-and-spoke structure pioneered by FedEx. Take a look at the route map in the seat pocket in front of you; you'll see that your airline's system probably resembles a cascade of fireworks, with spokes radiating from one or more main hubs. Hub status can be a very important part of the

economy of a city, as large airlines create hundreds of thousands of jobs and invest billions of dollars around their hubs. In this photo, you can see a concentration of hotels, warehouses, support buildings, and other ancillary businesses to the northwest of the airport itself.

into an undifferentiated shallow lake. Watch especially for lines of trees, buildings, and roadways poking out of the water in flooded areas. The river's meanders, the side channels, and the floodplain itself provide immense water-storage capacity in the Mississippi Embayment. The complexity of the waterways in the embayment not only keeps the area moist and fertile but also moderates the effects of massive floods and prevents the obliteration of downstream cities like New Orleans.

Abundant wetlands also make this a prime habitat for birds. Combined with the north-south orientation of the river, these wetlands make the Mississippi Flyway the most heavily traveled in North America. Millions of birds—including waterfowl like ducks and geese and smaller birds like blackbirds, warblers, and sparrows—use it each year to migrate between overwintering areas in Central America, the Caribbean, and the Gulf of Mexico and summer breeding grounds in the Midwest, the Great Lakes, the taiga, and the Arctic.

The floodplain also makes for ideal farmland (when it isn't flooded), and you'll see plenty of agriculture here, much of it devoted to cotton, rice, and corn. The Mississippi is also an important industrial corridor. It carries half a billion tons of cargo each year, but on long barges rather than the riverboats of Mark Twain's day. You'll probably see some as you fly over—watch for long, rectangular shapes, often strung together like aquatic trains.

Three miles (5 km) under the Mississippi Embayment is a half-billion-year-old continental rift known as a graben. In 1811 and 1812, the most severe earthquakes known to have hit North America took place here, along the New Madrid Fault. Hundreds of people died or lost their homes in spite of the very sparse settlement at the time. Three quakes, each ten times more powerful than the one that leveled San Francisco almost a century later, sent the Mississippi over its banks and were felt in the coastal cities of the Eastern Seaboard as far north as Boston. Today, tens of millions of people live along the Mississippi Embayment, oblivious to the several small but ominous quakes here each week.

WATCH FOR:

GEOLOGICAL Features	HYDROLOGICAL Features	ECOLOGICAL Features	HUMAN Features
Salt domes	The Mississippi Delta	Bayous	Oil and gas wells and platforms
	Beaches	Swamps	Canals
	Gulf of Mexico		Fishing boats
			French long lots

BONUS SIGHTS: Shrimp boats, Lake Ponchartrain.

While flying over the Gulf Coast you may notice that it looks similar to the Southern Coastal Plain. But a very different geology lies underneath. An ancient ocean met its demise here, drying up and leaving thick deposits of salt that were later covered by layers of sedimentary rock.

Just because you can't see the salt doesn't mean it's not there. Under pressure, salt liquefies and forms underground upwellings called salt domes—features also found under the Colorado Plateau (see page 107). These domes often collect petroleum in the rock around them, and so are of great interest to oil companies—wellheads often indicate the presence of a salt dome deep underground.

The wells tap into deposits of oil and gas, both on land and off-shore, and are a major component of the local economy. You can spot oil and gas fields easily: Watch for groups of small dirt roads or canals leading to areas of cleared ground. The wells are in the clearings, and they are connected by pipelines and pumping stations. You can gauge a field's richness by the density of these features. Offshore, look for square platforms rising out of the Gulf.

You'll also see plenty of evidence of fishing, another key piece of the economy here. The warm coastal waters and swampy shores provide abundant habitat for fish and shrimp, and you'll notice trawlers moving back and forth across the shallows. Behind each one trails a brown plume of sediment pulled up from the bottom. Unfortunately, heavy fishing here has severely disrupted the local marine ecosystems, as virtually every part of the inshore seabed has been dragged again and again.

A SALT DOME ⊱ The West Hackberry Salt Dome, its shape revealed by the canals and pipelines above it **1**, lies hundreds of feet under the Mississippi Delta south of Lake Charles, Louisiana. In the bayous, most of the roads and canals you will see are associated with oil and gas exploration. Along with three other salt domes in Texas and Louisiana, West Hackberry has been part of the Department of Energy's Strategic Petroleum Reserve since the energy crisis of the 1970s. More than fifty caverns 200 feet wide and 2,000 feet tall (61 m by 610 m) have been dug into the salt, and each holds up to a day's worth of petroleum for the entire nation, making this the largest stockpile of crude oil in the world. Intended to provide petroleum for the nation in the event of another fuel shortage, the reserve contains half a billion barrels, enough oil to replace imports for about two months.

The large canal to the north of the reserve **2** is part of the Intracoastal Waterway. Canals require constant maintenance, but they make water travel much easier and more efficient in this area. Note how the natural system resists the engineers' straight lines, turning the canals back into meanders wherever given the chance.

The Mississippi Delta

The Mississippi Delta you can see from the air is actually just the top of a mountain of sediment that the great river has carried out of the heart of the North American continent over the last sixty million years.

The mud you see here, once part of the Rockies and the Appalachians, is the exposed tip of an enormous cone-shaped pile of sediment 40,000 feet (12 km) thick—higher than your plane's cruising altitude—extending 300 miles (480 km) from the coast on the floor of the Gulf.

Geologically, this is one of the most dynamic areas of the continent, changing fast enough to be easily observed over the course of a human

THE MISSISSIPPI DELTA ⊱ Around the town of Thibodaux **1** in the heart of the Mississippi Delta, French long lots on either side of Bayou Lafourche **2** date back more than two centuries. This system gave each farmer both fertile land and access to the river for irrigation and transportation. Where the lots are extremely narrow, they have been divided lengthwise under French inheritance custom.

A bayou is a sluggish channel of freshwater in the flat delta. Beyond the settled fields are marshy cypress swamps—sodden forests of tall, buttressed cypress, mangroves, and Spanish moss.

Louisiana contains 40 percent of the wetlands in the conterminous United States, but these wetlands are being lost at a disturbing rate. Channelization and other human modifications have upset the natural dynamism of the Mississippi Delta: nearly 1 million acres (405,000 ha) of wetland may be lost here in the next few decades, allowing seawater to encroach 30 miles (50 km) or more, wiping out towns like Thibodaux.

lifetime. Variations in the river course farther upstream create dramatic changes at its mouth, where seven subdeltas—look for muddy lobes riddled with channels leading out to the Gulf—have been established in succession over the past five thousand years. Were it not for continuous, difficult, and expensive intervention by the U.S. Army Corps of Engineers, which maintains a huge system of levees, canals, and other waterworks here, the Mississippi River would today enter the Gulf 100 miles (160 km) farther west. Watch for large canals and levees—long, straight mounds that contain the river course—locked in battle with the whims of the Big Muddy.

Were the river's course to change, the foundation of New Orleans' economy would disappear overnight. But ironically, the measures that prevent this from happening cause problems of their own. Without annual floods to replenish the silt on this soft terrain, the Big Easy is sinking; parts are already 10 feet (3 m) or more below sea level, making Louisiana the only state besides California with dry (for now) land lower than the ocean. While all cities, and indeed all human structures, are due one day to be obliterated by unstoppable geological forces, New Orleans' moment of truth is far more imminent than most.

THE VIEW AT NIGHT

Virtually all the light you see on the ground comes from human activity—at night, the ground below becomes a life-size map of the human realm.

The density of light, corresponding to the concentration of human endeavor, makes visible the grand patterns of organization. Networks of roads and towns strung across the Great Plains grow closer and bigger before finally merging into Chicago's illuminated expanse, while lonely outposts shine in the High Arctic darkness with a single bright light.

The nightscape is a combination of points of white and orange. Orange lights improve contrast for nighttime drivers, are more energy efficient, and produce less light pollution—scattered, hazy light that obscures the night sky.

Other than electric lights, you may see the flares of gases being burned off at oil refineries, landfills, and gas fields, and the occasional forest fire. The rest is inky darkness (see pages 154–55 and page 160 for information about atmospheric lights).

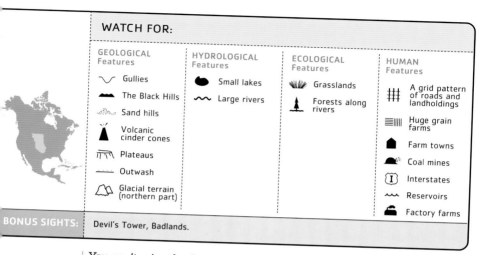

WATCH FOR:

GEOLOGICAL Features	HYDROLOGICAL Features	ECOLOGICAL Features	HUMAN Features
⌄ Gullies	🌑 Small lakes	🌿 Grasslands	⌗ A grid pattern of roads and landholdings
▲ The Black Hills	〰 Large rivers	🌲 Forests along rivers	≡‖ Huge grain farms
Sand hills			⬢ Farm towns
▲ Volcanic cinder cones			⬛ Coal mines
⋔ Plateaus			① Interstates
— Outwash			〜 Reservoirs
△ Glacial terrain (northern part)			⬛ Factory farms

BONUS SIGHTS: Devil's Tower, Badlands.

You can't miss the Great Plains: Every coast-to-coast flight passes over them, and their expansiveness is a startling contrast to the rest of the continent. The western edge of the Great Plains features the most dramatic and unmistakable boundary between regions in North America. After climbing for 300 miles (480 km) from the banks of the Missouri, the Great Plains come to an abrupt halt at the foot of the Rocky Mountains. Watch for the north-south lines of hogback escarpments that mark the transition between regions: Hogback escarpments are the upturned edges of the sedimentary rock that underlies all of the Great Plains—watch for sharp north-south ridges of reddish-brown rock jutting abruptly from the plains.

If you're flying any of the numerous routes through Denver, you'll get a chance to see this border close up, as Denver is at the very edge of the Great Plains where the Rockies loom like a solid wall. If you're flying over without stopping, you might feel it: This transition causes turbulence as winds plunge eastward into the Great Plains, creating waves in the atmosphere like the rush of water above a rock in a streambed (see page 159 for more information about the atmosphere).

The undulating hills and flat plateaus you're looking down on have had more or less the same topography for seventy million years, since the demise of a shallow sea that separated the western and eastern

SALINA, KANSAS ➤ This picture sums up much of what you'll see in the wetter, more intensively cultivated part of the Great Plains, east of the 100th meridian. Founded as a jumping-off point for prospectors traveling west in search of gold, Salina grew quickly after the Union Pacific Railroad came to town in 1867. It is still centered around a rail terminal **1**. Look for arrays of grain silos standing like giant batteries in the middle of railyards. This focus on transportation was reinforced by more modern developments: the classic cloverleaf where I-70 meets I-135 **2** and the regional airport **3**.

The compact downtown near the rail terminal eventually gave way to more sprawling development **4**, where new subdivisions occupy entire sections of the grid (see page 82 for more information about the grid and page 52 for more information about sprawl). But the natural features of the Great Plains are still there: Faint patterns of oxbows and the meanders of Spring Creek are visible near the channelized modern river **5**, as are intriguing crop marks and broad drainage patterns revealed in the different crops around the town.

halves of North America. This sea left behind thick sediments, sometimes more than 10,000 feet (3 km) deep. Consolidated into sedimentary rock (limestone, shale, and others), these layers are occasionally punctured by intrusions of the granite that underlies most of the northern

HIGH PLAINS RANGELAND ⏵ This view shows the typical drainage pattern of feathery branching gullies cut into the prairie on the border of Nebraska and South Dakota. The more sheltered, wetter environment is ideal for tree growth, but between these drainages you can see classic prairie grassland. **1** In the north, heavily eroded Badlands **2** are visible as white patches. This is the terrain on which millions of bison once roamed, and across which the nomadic Sioux and other indigenous peoples traveled. Today, the bison are gone, replaced by more docile cattle, and the Sioux are confined to destitution on reservations like Pine Ridge, which extends northward from this image.

part of the continent. Occasionally, particularly in the northern reaches of the Great Plains, this harder rock breaks through with dramatic results, including Devil's Tower in Wyoming and South Dakota's Black Hills—these small, isolated mountain ranges, with their sharp peaks

1mi

1km

A FEEDLOT ≻ This immense facility (the Monfort Feedlot, owned by ConAgra, the second-largest U.S. food company) is a collection point for beef from all over the High Plains. Every day, thousands of cattle are brought here to be fattened up on a rich diet of grain, antibiotics, and protein supplements, then slaughtered in the giant abattoir in the center of the feedlot before being butchered on high-speed assembly lines. Cuts of meat are sent to supermarkets and restaurants around the country. Because of the dense concentration of animals, a feedlot's water consumption and effluent is comparable to that of a city, endangering the South Platte River.

Throughout agricultural areas of the country, you'll also be able to spot modern industrial chicken and pig farms. Look for rows of long, low metal sheds next to dark, square cesspools. The animals live densely packed in the sheds and their waste is stored in the fetid pools.

Massive centralization has taken place in many sectors of American industry since World War II. Look for very large buildings between major markets with prominent transportation links.

and forested valleys, are a stark contrast with the flat grasslands around them.

Rivers flowing out of the mountains to the west first deposited sediment here and then cut the channels you see. These channels, and the plateaus between them, are all of relatively recent origin: They were created over the course of the last two million years or so.

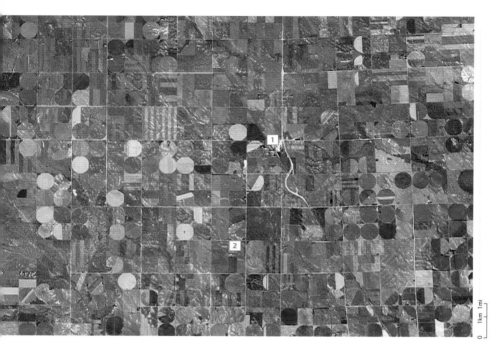

HIGH PLAINS AGRICUL-
TURE ⊱ The tiny town of
Hemingford, Nebraska
1, population 963 (about
the same as a couple of
fully loaded jumbo jets), a
transfer point where grain
is moved onto a rail spur,
is nearly lost among the
ubiquitous circles created
by pivot irrigation (here
used to water corn). A well
at the center of each circle
pumps water through a
long, wheeled pipe that
rotates like the glowing
arm on an old-fashioned
radar screen.

Throughout the Great
Plains, water is drawn from
the Oglala aquifer, a vast
and ancient underground
reservoir. Unfortunately,
the intensity of irrigation
here removes water from
the aquifer far faster than
it is returned (25,000
such circles can be found
in Nebraska alone), threat-
ening the future of this
great agricultural region.
In contrast, dryland
farming, here of wheat
and soy, relies on rainfall.
The alternating stripes in
some fields are a means
of erosion control called
strip-cropping, in which
different plants are grown
side by side. Farther east,
where erosion due to water
runoff is a greater concern,
you'll see the graceful
swirls of contour cropping,
in which different crops
are planted in strips per-
pendicular to the slope
of the land.

As usual in the West,
human land use is marked
by the orderly grid, with the
larger pivot systems each
occupying a quarter section
(see page 82 for more
information about the grid).
Subtle variations in crop
coloration (crop marks)
reveal underlying patterns
in the landscape that affect
soil moisture, such as
ancient dunes, variations in
bedrock, or evidence of
past human activity. In this
case, the crop marks run
diagonally with the area's
natural drainage, in parallel
with Hemingford Creek **2**
just south of the town.

Immense herds of animals made these vast and easily traveled plains their home. Uncountable numbers of triceratops once roamed hot, swampy woodlands—forests that are now the rich coalfields of the High Plains (the western and northern parts of the Great Plains—watch for the rounded or squarish black scars of open-pit coal mines and long, sinuous coal trains here). Later, exotic mammals like horses, camels, and tapirs—as well as gigantic creatures like the moropus, a cousin of the rhinoceros, and titanotheres, a beast with long, curved horns on its snout—filled these steppes in the millions. More recently, seemingly limitless herds of bison trod these lands. But they, too, met their match: The westward spread of modern civilization put an end to the roaming herds that, in one form or another, had occupied these lands for nearly one hundred million years. Today, cattle graze this rangeland in domesticated imitation of the great herds.

The natural ecosystem prior to the arrival of European settlers was semiarid grassland, with narrow bands of trees (known as riparian forest) hugging the rivers. Ideal for cultivating grains, the Great Plains became America's agricultural heartland, churning out the meat and potatoes of the American diet. Nearly everywhere you look, you'll see farms growing wheat, soybeans, and corn and feedlots, grain elevators, and cattle yards.

The transformation of the Great Plains from wild grassland to the breadbasket of North America came about through an unfortunate history of displacement. Today, the names of the indigenous inhabitants are spread like ghosts across the landscape, attached to towns, mountains, and rivers. As the forces of expansion confined these peoples to reservations and exterminated the hordes of bison, the landscape changed dramatically. Hardscrabble European immigrants tilled the native soil and created a new civilization: an image of Europe recast for a new continent. These are the towns and farms you see beneath you today.

"The West" begins in the Great Plains. The 100th meridian, at the east edge of the Texas Panhandle, is generally considered the dividing line, for this is roughly the farthest west that crops thrive without irrigation. This is where you will see the fields transition from square to round: the telltale sign of pivot irrigation.

In the Great Plains you'll see the immense scale of American agriculture. Farms are huge—often an entire section of the grid—and are heavily mechanized. This agriculture depends on the modern petroleum economy not only to drive the machines of transportation and harvest, but also to manufacture the fertilizers, pesticides, and herbicides that are the hallmark of this sort of massive monoculture (large areas growing just one crop). Because this technology allows farm workers to be highly productive, agriculture—this huge feature of the view from the air—employs just 2 percent of the American workforce.

All the basics of the American diet are grown here: potatoes, wheat, corn, soy, pigs, chickens, and cattle. Besides the endless fields, look for the telltale buildings that support this endeavor: tall grain elevators near rail lines, rows of low metal sheds where pigs and chickens are raised, and processing plants where animals are slaughtered and food is prepared for shipment out to the world.

THE GRID

In the nineteenth century, the Cartesian ideal of geometric perfection served as the foundation for all land planning in the United States. The grid carved out of the prairie or gloomy forest bespoke the orderly hand of rational man on the disordered wildness of nature. It permitted distant planners to parcel out land to settlers in a hurry, and it evoked solidity and permanence—a scaffolding—for an inchoate nation.

From the Atlantic Ocean to Ohio, the older towns and countryside of the East reflect the more chaotic patterns of the European tradition,

conforming to the realities of landform. Starting west of Ohio, in 1785, the federal government surveyed the nation into a grid of (mostly) perfect squares 6 miles (9.7 km) on each side. These Congressional or Survey "townships" were further divided into 36 "sections" a mile (1.6 km) on each side.

If you are flying west of Ohio and see land that is clearly laid out in anything other than a grid, you are looking at the handiwork of previous colonial authorities: Spanish in the Southwest and California, British and French in the Great lakes region, and French in Louisiana.

In the Midwest, townships can be seen as the grid of larger county roads atop the grid of smaller farm roads and fields. Sections, half-sections, quarter-sections, and so on define the shapes and sizes of many farms in the Midwest and Great Plains.

In the West, sections can be seen as forest and range landholdings in an alternating, checkerboard pattern, as seen below in the Klamath National Forest in Northern California. These lands were granted to states and railroads by the federal government to offset the costs of development. Different land-use practices in adjacent parcels have created a dramatic checkerboard that can be seen very clearly in many places.

If you spot two grids coming together unevenly, then you have found the boundary between two regions that were surveyed starting from different points (these transitions are often the boundary between states or territories).

Klamath National Forest

Because the grid is so regular, you can use it to estimate your plane's ground speed. Just lean your head up against the window so it's stationary, and put your fingertip on the window where you can see it. As the sectional lines of the grid pass your finger, count how many seconds it takes to go from one line to the next (this works best if you are flying north-south or east-west). Do this a few times to get an average. That number is the time it takes for you to travel one mile in seconds. To convert to miles per hour, just divide 3600 (the number of seconds in an hour) by the number of seconds you counted. To convert to kilometers per hour, just divide 5800 by the number you counted. So, if you counted 8 seconds between major grid lines, then your ground speed is 450 miles per hour (725 km/h).

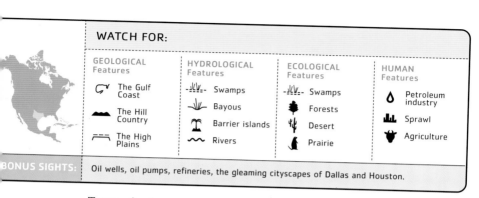

WATCH FOR:

GEOLOGICAL Features	HYDROLOGICAL Features	ECOLOGICAL Features	HUMAN Features
⌒ The Gulf Coast	Swamps	Swamps	◊ Petroleum industry
The Hill Country	Bayous	Forests	Sprawl
The High Plains	Barrier islands	Desert	Agriculture
	Rivers	Prairie	

BONUS SIGHTS: Oil wells, oil pumps, refineries, the gleaming cityscapes of Dallas and Houston.

Texas, the largest state in the lower forty-eight, is a meeting place where the Great Plains, the desert, and the Gulf Coast abut one another. The sweltering coastal swamps near Houston give way quickly as the

FREDERICKSBURG, TEXAS ⤳ German settlers laid out Fredericksburg like the towns they knew in their homeland: A broad main street running parallel to a river, as can be seen in this image. The Hill Country, a region of forested hills where the High Plains drop toward the Coastal Plain, lies between the humidity of the coast and the dry interior, so the climate favors agriculture.

land rises in the west toward the High Plains. In the south, the state turns into a parched northern extension of the Chihuahua Desert.

Texas is the only state in the continental United States that functioned as an independent republic, and its brashly distinctive culture combines the genteel but finicky charm of the Old South, the spontaneity

0 1km 1mi

SAN ANTONIO, TEXAS ⤖ San Antonio, at the foot of the Edwards Plateau and the Great Plains, has one of the most violent histories of all North American cities. Originally the site of a Spanish mission, the city has been invaded several times by various armies: It is here, for example, that the Alamo, a mission occu-

pied by a small force of Texan separatist settlers fighting for independence from Spain, fell to the Mexican army in 1836.

Today, however, peace reigns and the city is the third largest in Texas. It is also a perfect example of unimpeded twentieth-century sprawl. With a compact center of office

towers near its original locus, the city is low and spread out, with a series of circular ring roads. This layout, made possible by the automobile, paradoxically also requires cars for easy navigation (see page 52 for more information about sprawl).

and individualism of the West, and the flamboyant traditionalism of northern Mexico. But from the air, the most apparent Texan hallmark is oil.

Watch for the wells themselves: From high altitudes, you'll notice networks of access roads leading to wellheads, and at lower heights you may be able to see the pumps themselves, bobbing like rocking horses. You'll also spot other elements of the oil industry, particularly refineries along the Gulf Coast: Look for large industrial installations with lots of pipes next to fields of huge cylindrical tanks. At night, amid bril-

1mi
1km

0

LA FRONTERA ≻ Eagle Pass, Texas, on the right and Piedras Negras, Coahuila, form a single conurbation on either side of the Rio Grande/Rio Bravo between the United States and Mexico. Pairs of twin towns and cities are strung all along the border, about half of which is in Texas. The border is almost 2,000 miles (3,200 km) long and crosses some extremely inhospitable territory.

Trade—legal or not— has always been the main activity at these border crossings. The border zone has been growing quickly in recent decades, particularly on the Mexican side, as special regulations allow factories here to take advantage of cheaper Mexican workers and laxer environmental and labor regulations without sacrificing access to the lucrative U.S. market.

liantly lit complexes, you'll see the bright orange flames of gases being burned off from their smokestacks.

In the twentieth century, oil transformed Texas from a rural backwater to a dynamic giant with a diversified economy that has led the nation in job growth since 1990. You'll see signs of this growth all over the state, but particularly in the east, where the cities are ringed in expanding suburbs, complete with subdivisions, office parks, malls, and freeways.

ENERGY

Whether we're using an electric light, driving a car, flying a plane, refining aluminum, or making fertilizers, everything we do requires energy. It's not surprising that the massive infrastructure providing this power is visible nearly everywhere.

From the air, you'll see hydroelectric dams, which create large reservoirs of water (branching lakes with one flat end; see page 103) in order to drive their turbines, as well

An oil and gas field

An oil refinery

as coal mines (open pits of black) and oil and gas fields, like the one on page 87, just outside Taft, California.

Watch for the telltale network of dirt roads leading to clearings around each wellhead. Oil is collected from the wells and pumped to the tanks visible in the image on page 87. This example is part of the Elk Hills Naval Petroleum Reserve, a legacy from before World War I, and is a very rich field, dense with wells; in other areas, you may see them much more spread out (see the photo on page 144).

From the well, petroleum is moved to refineries, where it is separated into useful substances like gasoline, jet fuel, heating oil, and the raw materials for plastics. Texas City, on the Gulf Coast, is home to seven major refineries, including this BP-Amoco facility (above)—the city's largest employer and, with the capacity to process half a million barrels of crude each day, the third-largest refinery in the United States.

Electrical energy—the form of power we use the most for everything other than transportation—is generated at centralized plants (although solar and wind facilities are a little more spread out—as you'll see if you fly over the fields of windmills outside San Francisco or Los Angeles).

The Callaway Nuclear Power Plant (below), outside Fulton, Missouri, is one of the 104 commercial nuclear power plants in the United States. Callaway's concrete cooling tower is typical of U.S. nuclear plants. The reactor itself is in the domed structure in the middle of the facility.

Most power plants sit close to bodies of water used for cooling. In this case, the plant pumps water from the Missouri River, 5 miles (8 km) south of the site.

You can identify generating plants of all kinds by watching for the high-voltage power lines that emanate from them. Watch for straight corridors cut through forests, up and over hills, and through cities and towns (see the photos on pages 35, 45, and 46).

With the exception of hydro-electric, solar, geothermal, and wind generation, all our modes of power production create a great deal of waste. From your window you'll see this waste as smog and plumes from smokestacks, and, if you're in the right place in the Great Basin, you might spot the national nuclear-waste storage site at Yucca Mountain, an otherwise undistinguished ridge near Las Vegas.

A nuclear power plant

ED STATES THE WE

TED STATES THE U

UNITED STATES T

N UNITED STATES

CANADA

Seattle •

**Pacific
Northwest**

Rockies

San Francisco •

California

Deserts

• Denver

USA

Las Vegas •

Los Angeles •

Phoenix •

Pacific Ocean

MEXICO

THE WESTERN UNITED STATES

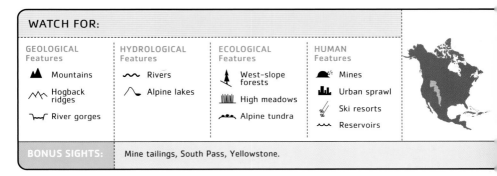

WATCH FOR:

GEOLOGICAL Features	HYDROLOGICAL Features	ECOLOGICAL Features	HUMAN Features
▲▲ Mountains	∿ Rivers	▲ West-slope forests	▰ Mines
⋀⋀ Hogback ridges	⋀⌣ Alpine lakes	▥ High meadows	▟▙▄ Urban sprawl
⌐⌐ River gorges		⋏⋏ Alpine tundra	⚞ Ski resorts
			∿∿ Reservoirs

BONUS SIGHTS: Mine tailings, South Pass, Yellowstone.

The Rocky Mountains' high peaks—rocky gray in summer and snow-capped in winter—are an unmistakable feature of our continent, especially when you're flying west. Rising abruptly from the Great Plains, this daunting wall of rock presented a formidable physical barrier to westward expansion of the United States; the great Continental Divide passes through these mountains. This is the line that separates rivers flowing to the Atlantic and Arctic Oceans from those that end in the Pacific and that signals the beginning of a different kind of country.

Extending from the Mackenzie Delta in the High Arctic to southern Mexico, the North American Cordillera, of which the Rockies are a part, was formed forty million to eighty million years ago as the North American Plate met the Pacific Plate in a tectonic collision (see page 32 for more information about plate tectonics).

The resulting upheaval threw mountains up from what had been swampy lowlands and shallow seas. These areas were rich with dinosaurs including the apatosaurus, one of the largest land animals ever, and other old favorites like the stegosaurus and the allosaurus, making this region today one of the world's best hunting grounds for dinosaur fossils. The sedimentary limestone, shale, chalk, and sandstone created over the eons thrust skyward, fracturing to create a sharp, craggy mountain range.

Millions of years of erosion washed this material down into the Great Plains and the Mississippi Basin, leaving behind the rugged granite base rock we see today.

BOULDER, COLORADO ➤ The Front Range **1** brings the sprawl emanating from Boulder to a halt. Note the darker forest cover replacing the lighter scrub and grassland as the elevation rises suddenly to the west. In the mountains you can see the twisting roads of new development, a more exclusive form of sprawl with a much better view and different challenges (see page 52 for more information about sprawl and page 97 for more information about forest fires).

Veins of metal ores run through the rock, making these mountains more than just an obstacle to settlers. A gold rush in 1858 that led to the founding of both Denver and Colorado Springs has left its mark on the land. This area is a major crossing point for east-west air traffic, so watch for mine tailings as you cross the Front Range (the steep wall of mountains west of Denver). Mine tailings here usually appear as uneven and lightly vegetated rubble tumbling down from holes in the mountains.

Colorado is again developing rapidly, now the third-fastest-growing state. From the air, the signs are abundant: New roads, subdivisions, industrial installations, malls, and of course airports litter the piedmont north and south of Denver. Parts of this area grew by 200 percent in the 1990s (see page 52 for more information about urban sprawl).

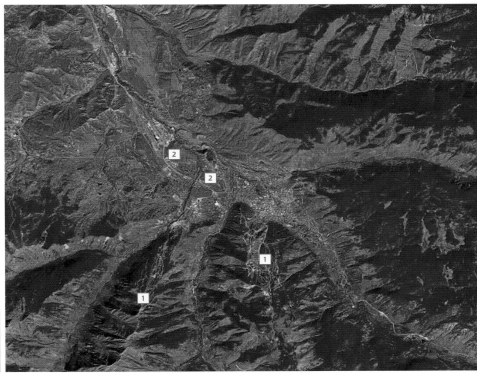

ASPEN, COLORADO ➤
Aspen is a lovely place—
you can ski right into the
center of town. The cleared
areas winding up the mountainsides **1** are ski runs,
and in the winter you may
even be able to spot skiers
against the bright white
snow. Aspen is one of the
most expensive towns in
the country, and suffers a
severe shortage of afford-
able housing. Many of
the people who clean and
cook, or run chair lifts in the
resort areas, must commute
for hours over dangerous
mountain roads as a result.
Note the golf courses in the
valley **2**, which, along with
smaller details like tennis
courts and swimming pools,
are indications of affluence.
Aspen is on the Great
Divide: Just to the east,
on the other side of the
Sawatch Range, the head-
waters of the Arkansas
River flow eastward, but
Roaring Fork River, flowing
north through Aspen,
joins the westward-flowing
Colorado River a few miles
from here.

To the west of the Front Range, you'll see that the character of
the mountains changes and becomes less craggy and more rounded—
evidence of heavy glaciation over the past two million years. Most of
the settlements you'll see here were once mining towns but are now picturesque, and often very expensive, resorts like Aspen and Vail.

Because of North America's prevailing west-to-east weather pattern, the western slope of the Rockies is much wetter than the semiarid eastern slope (see page 164 for more information about weather). As you cross the mountains from East to West, you can see this in the form of denser vegetation: forests instead of the dry steppes of the High Plains. In the transition zone, watch for trees hugging the more sheltered north sides of mountains and ridges. You'll also see that at higher elevations the mountains support only very limited vegetation because of the cold climate above the treeline.

To the north, in Wyoming, you may fly over South Pass—the only break in the Cordillera between the Arctic Ocean and Mexico's Sierra Madre range. South Pass was the main route for wagon trains in their journey to settle out West. Fort Laramie, at the east end of the pass, was the staging point for the beginning of the arduous trek through the mountains along the Oregon Trail. In 1869 the Union Pacific Railroad opened the first transcontinental railway through here, and even today the nation's main east-west surface artery, Interstate 80, cuts through South Pass. If you're flying across the continent nonstop, you're likely to pass over this very area yourself. Watch for the roads and rail lines coming out of the pass and marvel at how much of an improvement air travel is over wagon trains.

Yellowstone

North of the pass is the Yellowstone caldera, the end of an arc of giant volcanoes whose geothermal activity provides the basis for the famous park here (the first U.S. national park, established in 1872). Situated directly atop the Continental Divide, Yellowstone's waters (including huge Yellowstone Lake itself) have the distinction of flowing to both the Atlantic and Pacific Oceans.

The lakes here are notable from the air because they are among the largest natural bodies of water you'll see in these mountains. Most "lakes" here are actually reservoirs, with a telltale branching shape, but natural lakes like Yellowstone Lake are rounded (see page 103 for more information about water systems).

FOREST FIRES

Millions of acres of evergreen forest grow between the Front Range of the Rockies and the Coast Range on the Pacific. For thousands of years, the forest here featured large, widely spaced conifer trees interspersed with grassland and smaller trees. Light summertime fires burned through and renewed the grasslands. Indigenous people often set fires to improve habitat for game such as deer.

During most of the twentieth century, however, land managers saw fire as a wasteful impediment to the growth of valuable timber and suppressed the fires. As a result, the forest became closed and dense as trees filled in the formerly open spaces. The survival of many smaller, often sickly trees meant that when a fire did get going, it very quickly turned into a disaster, burning millions of acres in uncontrollable conflagrations.

In an effort to restore native ecosystems and reduce fire danger, some jurisdictions are now following a let-burn policy. When this strategy was first attempted in Yellowstone National Park in 1988, many viewed it as a catastrophe, but dramatic regeneration has vindicated the decision.

Elsewhere, human habitation makes this solution impossible. Notice how many homes are in the forests and along ridgetops outside the towns you pass (see the photo on page 94). For the most part, these developments have been built in the past several decades, and, while they may have magnificent views, fresh air, and peace and quiet, they are all at very high risk from fire.

If you're flying during the summer, you may even see a wildfire (check regional news reports before you fly so you'll know where to look); watch for plumes of whitish smoke rising from forestland, such as you can see in the photo on page 106. The smoke travels great distances, so when you spot smoke (usually either spread out like a low, dirty stratus cloud or billowing upward), try to follow it back to its source: That's a wildfire.

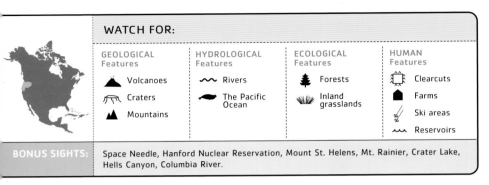

WATCH FOR:

GEOLOGICAL Features	HYDROLOGICAL Features	ECOLOGICAL Features	HUMAN Features
▲ Volcanoes	∿ Rivers	🌲 Forests	Clearcuts
Craters	The Pacific Ocean	Inland grasslands	⬠ Farms
▲ Mountains			Ski areas
			∿ Reservoirs

BONUS SIGHTS: Space Needle, Hanford Nuclear Reservation, Mount St. Helens, Mt. Rainier, Crater Lake, Hells Canyon, Columbia River.

The Pacific Northwest is rich and varied. Home to both rainforests and arid farmland, it's the start of a rugged meeting between ocean and mountains that stretches all the way to Alaska.

An ongoing collision between the North American and Pacific tectonic plates has, over the past thirty million years, pushed these mountains up. Melted pieces of the subducted (pushed-under) plate have resulted in very active—even explosive—geological events in this area (see page 32 for more information about plate tectonics).

The Cascades

The Cascade Mountains are one example of this. Stretching north to south just inland from the coast, this chain of volcanoes includes Mount Rainier, Mount Saint Helens, Mount Hood, and Mount Shasta.

From Lassen Peak in California to Mount Garibaldi in British Columbia, the Cascades include more than twenty active volcanoes, many over 10,000 feet (3,000 m) high. Underneath each one—a mile or more down—is a chamber of hot molten rock that powers volcanic eruptions. These mountains lie above an arc of molten rock that bursts through the crust of the North American Plate in catastrophic volcanic explosions. Seven have erupted in the past 200 years, with the most recent being Mount Saint Helens in 1980; that explosion sent a plume of gas and smoke 60,000 feet into the air and rained ash as far as North Dakota.

And the eruptions can get much bigger: Nearly eight thousand years ago, Mount Mazama, in southern Oregon, exploded with fifty times the power of Mount Saint Helens' most recent eruption. Its upper

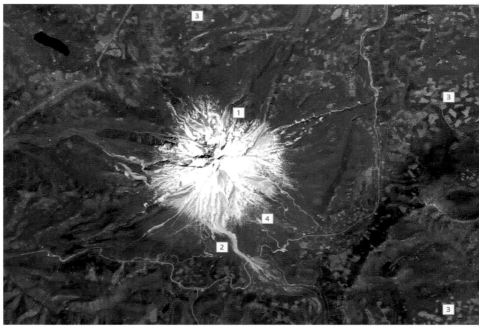

MOUNT HOOD ⊱ Mount Hood, a classic volcanic cone 11,237 feet (3,425 m) high, sits 50 miles (80 km) east of Portland, Oregon, in the center of the Cascades, a chain of more than twenty active volcanoes, including Mount Saint Helens and Mount Shasta. Mount Hood last erupted in 1865, and has been shaped by glaciers, water, lava, and mud-flows. In particular, note the lava flows toward the northeast **1** and the mud-flow that heads south **2** toward the White River.

The mountain is a designated wilderness area within the Mount Hood National Forest, which also features hundreds of clearcuts **3**, a typical characteristic of National Forest lands in the West. Lighter patches indicate more recent cuts. The patchy area to the southeast of the peak is a ski area **4**, one of more than 130 operated on U.S. Forest Service land by private companies under 40-year permits. While ski areas are ecologically no friendlier than clearcuts, they provide recreation to 25 million people each year.

reaches were completely obliterated, leaving behind the caldera that is now Crater Lake. A conspicuously circular lake set within a collar of sharp peaks, it is quite easy to spot from the air.

The perfectly conical peaks of the Cascades are even more readily identified: They tower over neighboring mountains and are often covered with snow (indeed, Mount Shasta, in California, features some of the southernmost glaciers in the United States).

OLYMPIC FORESTS ➤ The West is the home of the clearcut, an ecologically damaging but economically efficient total removal of trees from an area of forest. Until the 1960s, clearcuts often took the form of totally denuded sections of the grid (640 acres, or 259 ha). Today, these old cuts are visible as large, perfectly square

areas of uniform regrowth. Under stricter environmental regulations, modern clearcuts are more likely to be smaller and to conform to the landscape, as in this image. Look for triangle-shaped clearings that fan out from a single point—a landing, where the logs are loaded onto trucks. Also, watch for so-called "beauty strips" of untouched forest

that surround public roads through heavily logged areas and help limit public view of the devastation behind. The clearcuts in this image are in Olympic National Forest, while the protected Olympic National Park **1** includes the largest expanse of old-growth temperate rain forest in the continental United States.

The Temperate Rain Forest

The Pacific Northwest is world famous for its temperate rain forests, and you'll see plenty from the air, cloaking the mountainsides in a deep green blanket. Heavy rain, a mild climate, and coastal fog support the largest trees in the world, including coastal redwoods in California and Sitka spruce and western hemlocks farther north. Many of these trees reach heights of up to 300 feet (90 m) or more and some are more than a thousand years old. This unique ecosystem occurs in only a few small regions around the globe, and the expanse from Northern California to the Alaska Panhandle is the largest.

Until the 1980s, this part of the country was the largest producer of timber. Since then, restrictions on harvesting here and the exhaustion of marketable timber have made the Southeast the country's major timber region (see the photo on page 51).

Modern human populations are centered around Oregon's Willamette Valley (which includes Portland) and Puget Sound in Washington (including Seattle). Both areas are ideal for human settlement and feature rich farmland and sheltered ports. While both centers arose through exploitation of natural resources, in particular timber, fish, and farming, they now depend on the modern globalized economy and are home to corporate icons like Nike (Beaverton, outside Portland) and Microsoft (Redmond, near Seattle).

The Columbia Plateau

Farther inland, the forest thins out and the landscape becomes drier. You'll see an abrupt change as you fly east over the Cascades. This is the Columbia Plateau, a region that blends characteristics of the intermountain deserts, the Rockies, and the forestlands toward the coast (see page 97 for more information about the forests here).

The Columbia Plateau is a remnant of wave after wave of indescribably violent geological events. Massive volcanic eruptions between six and seventeen million years ago laid down hundreds of layers of lava, including one of the largest single flows known to have occurred on Earth.

The lava was scoured by Ice Age glaciers, which eventually created ancient Lake Missoula, a deep (2,000 ft., or 600 m) and voluminous (as much as Lake Erie and Lake Ontario combined) body of water in the area surrounding Spokane. When the ice dam that created the lake burst more than fifteen thousand years ago, the lakewater became a thundering wall of water, ice, and rock traveling 65 miles (105 km) per hour. Such flooding occurred again and again as the Ice Age glaciers waxed and waned for thousands of years, and, each time, the landscape was re-formed as gorges were created, huge boulders tumbled hither and yon, and outwash scablands were left behind.

The Snake River between Idaho and Washington and Oregon marks the eastern edge of the Columbia Plateau. Hells Canyon, on the Idaho

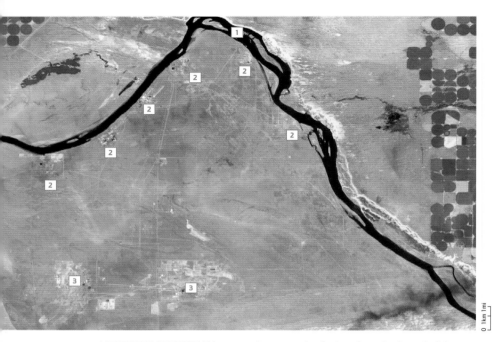

0 1 km 1 mi

ACCIDENTAL PROTECTION >— The northern edge of the Columbia Plateau opens onto the Columbia Basin in eastern Washington. Home to a unique meadow-steppe ecosystem, this area also hosts the Hanford Site, one of the most contaminated places in the nation and, ironically, one of its most pristine. Such potentially prime farm-land—note the intensive agriculture extending right to the area's boundary—has usually been the last to receive protection for its natural systems. But, with more than 500 square miles (1,300 sq. km) of native grassland along the free-flowing Columbia River **1**, this area has enjoyed the most rigorous protection possible—total exclusion of human use outside certain zones—since 1943, when it was selected to be the production facility for the nation's nuclear arsenal. It includes such rarities as the last salmon spawning grounds in the main channel of the Columbia, important migra-tory bird habitat, and the largest undisturbed semiarid steppe in North America. But it is also home to staggering amounts of highly radioactive and poisonous waste, including several old nuclear reactors **2** and their spent fuel, chemical processing plants **3**, and nearly two hundred giant (and leaking) under-ground storage tanks of liquid radioactive waste.

border, is the deepest river gorge in North America; the walls reach about 8,000 feet (2,400 m), tying with Kings Canyon in California. You might spot it from the air: Watch for a very deep and narrow north-south gorge with a raging river at the bottom.

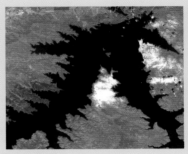

Fort Peck Lake

WATER SYSTEMS

The most immediately visible feature of water management on the landscape is the reservoir formed behind a dam. Watch for long, branched bodies of water with one conspicuously flat end—that's the dam. The water surface is flat, so the jaggedness of the shoreline is an indication of the ruggedness of the terrain around the dammed river course.

Dams and the reservoirs behind them provide water, flood control, aquatic recreation, and, in many cases, hydroelectric power, although they also disrupt river ecosystems.

Fort Peck Lake, shown here, is formed by the damming of the Missouri River in eastern Montana. The fifth-largest reservoir in the United States, it was flooded in the late 1930s to provide water for the West (and jobs during the Great Depression). Like most large public water-management systems in the United States, it is operated by the U.S. Army Corps of Engineers.

You are also likely to see canals during your flight. These long, narrow channels are used for navigation and water distribution, and are often connected to natural bodies of water (see pages 65, 73, and 135.) You'll see hundreds of miles of navigable canals in the Northeast and the Midwest, as well as in the Mississippi Basin and Florida, where people have con-structed navigable canals for almost 2,000 years.

Sewage-Treatment Facility

The California Aqueduct (below), which brings water to Los Angeles from the Sacramento–San Joaquin Delta, near San Francisco, snakes past housing developments and under the hills of the San Andreas Rift Zone on the outskirts of Palmdale, California. A major earthquake here could cut off much of the water that Los Angeles depends on.

Sewage-treatment plants are also important components of our water system. While hardly glamorous, the clusters of circular pools you'll see along waterways on the outskirts of any town or city in North America are crucial to maintaining the health of humans and nature alike.

Pictured above is the sewage-treatment facility of Des Moines, Iowa, downstream from the city on the Des Moines River. Wastewater is treated by filtration, bacterial fermentation, and chlorination before release into the river, free of most of the solids, bacteria, and chemicals that make sewage so objectionable.

The California Aqueduct

WATCH FOR:

GEOLOGICAL Features	HYDROLOGICAL Features	ECOLOGICAL Features	HUMAN Features
Canyons	Dry lake beds	Greenways along rivers and in washes	Mines
Outwash scrubland			Subdivisions
Sand dunes			Reservoirs
			Military bases

BONUS SIGHTS: Grand Canyon, Colorado River, Monument Valley, Painted Desert, Slot Canyons, Death Valley, Great Salt Lake, Las Vegas, Joshua trees, Amboy Crater, Lake Mead, and Lake Powell.

Home to stunning sights such as the Grand Canyon, the Painted Desert, and Monument Valley, the desert region is a visual feast from the air. The defining characteristic of any desert or semiarid region is limited rainfall—less than 20 inches (50 cm) each year. This is the fundamental parameter confronted by any living thing hoping to survive in the parched expanse stretching from central Mexico all the way to southern British Columbia. Some vegetation, like the cottonwood trees and mesquite scrub you can see hugging streambeds and depressions in the landscape, have adapted by growing only where there is some water all the time. You'll see that people take this approach, too: Most habitation in this region is near water.

Other organisms, like fairy shrimp and the desert wildflowers, whose springtime yellow and pink hues you may be able to see dusting the ground below you, are dormant and come to life only when it rains. Still others, such as cacti and desert tortoises, have specially adapted bodies that are extremely miserly with water. And others yet, such as migratory birds on the Pacific Flyway, stop through only to refresh themselves at the various widely spaced bodies of water on their way to greener pastures, just as you may be coming here simply to change planes. In the spring and fall, you might be able to spot large flocks of waterfowl moving across wet areas.

While life here is challenging, this is one of the most interesting parts of North America for aerial exploration. The limited rainfall and sparse human activity make flying over this region akin to surveying another planet, where the processes of raw geology are laid bare.

The deserts of the United States can be divided into four regions: the semiarid Colorado Plateau immediately to the west of the Rockies, which includes much of Colorado, New Mexico, Arizona, and Utah; the Great Basin, incorporating the rest of Utah and all of Nevada, as well as parts of Oregon and Idaho; the Mojave and Sonora Deserts in Southern California and Arizona; and, in southern New Mexico and far western Texas, a small piece of the Chihuahuan Desert (the largest in North America) extending northward from Mexico.

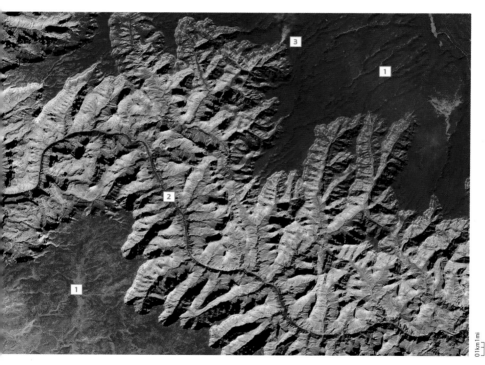

0 1 km 1 mi

THE GRAND CANYON ➤ The erosion that has taken place as the Colorado Plateau **1** has been up-lifted in the past 5 million years is nowhere more spectacular than at the

Grand Canyon, where the Colorado River **2** has carved one of the most magnificent gorges on Earth. Stretching for more than 200 miles (320 km) to the east of Las Vegas, the

Grand Canyon is 6,000 feet (1,829 m) deep and 18 miles (29 km) wide at its widest point. Note the plume of smoke from the small forest fire in this image **3**.

The Colorado Plateau

The Colorado Plateau is a layer cake of rock 3 miles (5 km) thick laid down over hundreds of millions of years. During its formation, it experienced nearly every type of landscape possible on Earth, including high mountains, warm seas, great sandy deserts, forestland, and swamps.

These layers continue to slowly rise, elevated by the motion of the Paradox Basin, a semiliquid layer of salt deep underground—the remnants of an ancient sea (see the photo on page 73). At the same time, over the past five million years, seasonal desert rains and the rivers they feed have eroded deep canyons in the rising plateau. You'll see many as you fly above this region; in particular watch for filigrees of very narrow slot canyons cut into the red rock.

The Grand Canyon, the greatest of these gorges, is unmistakable from the air. Resembling an inverted mountain range cut into the flat plateau, the canyon walls are ribboned with multicolored layers of rock laid down over the eons. The Precambrian basement rock at the very bottom, two billion years old, was once the foundation for a towering mountain range.

The Colorado Plateau is drained by the Colorado River, which originates on the western slopes of the Rockies. Colorado River water supplies farms and cities throughout the Southwest and northern Mexico, including expanding centers like Phoenix, Las Vegas, and Tijuana, as well as Los Angeles, the thirsty megacity that looms over all water in the western United States. The Colorado remains the subject of constant political squabbles and rivalries, as its water is the key constraint on human life in the arid West. The loser in these battles is always the river itself, which now no longer flows into the Sea of Cortez in Mexico but whimpers to a dry halt just south of the border.

Rugged and gorgeous, the Colorado Plateau is the stuff of classic western movies. The deep red of Navajo sandstone (legacy of a great sandy desert similar to the modern Sahara) is cut into the iconographic mesas of Monument Valley, the improbable-looking arches around Moab, the slot canyons of Escalante, and the otherworldly colors of the Painted Desert.

The Great Basin

The Great Basin starts off the western flank of the Wasatch Mountains in Utah, just to the west of Salt Lake City, and spreads west to the Sierra

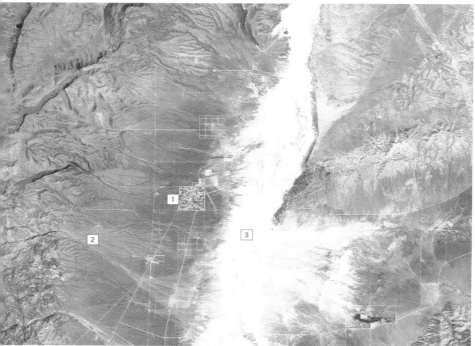

0 1km 1mi

BASIN AND RANGE ≻ The town of Crescent Valley **1** could be considered a god-forsaken mining outpost in the middle of nowhere (only 1,550 people live in the entire county). Sitting on an outwash plain (note the braided gullies at the opening of the drainages coming from the mountain range **2**) next to a playa— a perfectly flat, dry lake bed **3**—the area perfectly epitomizes the basin-and-range geology of Nevada.

Nevada. Here, you will see row after row of north-south mountain ranges separated by perfectly flat and dry ancient lakebeds. This landscape formed through the lifting and stretching force of melted pieces of the Pacific Plate rising beneath Earth's crust here, cracking the continental plate above. This represents one of the thinnest spots on Earth—as little as 13 miles (20 km) thick, just twice your plane's altitude.

Death Valley is one of these lakebeds. As the mountains are pulled apart, it sinks so much faster than it is filled by sedimentation that the valley floor is the lowest point in North America, as much as 282 feet (86 m) below sea level. Due to a rain shadow from the highest part of the Sierra Nevada, immediately to the west, Death Valley is bone dry

"THIS IS THE PLACE" ⟩— The south shore of the Great Salt Lake encapsulates modern human activity in the Great Basin. The suburbs of Salt Lake City and Provo sprawl into farmland to the east of this view. The Bingham Canyon open-pit copper mine **1**, is, after more than a century in operation, 2 miles wide and half a mile deep (3.2 km by 0.8 km), making it the largest excavation on the planet. Nearby, an ancient shoreline forms a bench partway up the mountains **2**.

Spotting the Great Salt Lake in 1847, Brigham Young declared, "This is the place," and so Salt Lake City was founded by Mormons migrating from persecution in the East. The Mormon City of Zion Plat, the model for town layouts here, features wide streets and an orderly grid, with a three-block civic center hosting a temple and civic buildings. There are more than 500 such settlements in the Great Basin, including Tooele **3**.

Equally precise in its layout is the Tooele Army Depot **4**, which stores materiel for the U.S. military, including chemical weapons. To the north, on the shore of the lake, evaporation ponds yield salt **5**. They are often reddish due to the presence of halophytic (salt-loving) red algae.

The following labels appear on the image: 2, 3, 1, 4, and a scale bar reading 1 km / 1 mi with 0.

THE AMBOY CRATER ➤ The perfect cinder cone of the Mojave Desert's Amboy Crater **1** rises 250 feet (75 m) from a lava field formed by a volcanic eruption 10,000 years ago. The tiny (and now privately owned) town of Amboy (population 20) is on Route 66 **2** , once the famous route west to California living. Amboy **3** is just 125 miles (200 km) from Los Angeles. Unlike the Eastern United States, where settlement sprawls with little geographical constraint, the West is a much harsher place, and sprawl can occur only where a sophisticated water-distribution system is in place (see page 52 for more information about sprawl and page 103 for more information about water systems). Salt evaporators **4** in the dry bed of Bristol Lake attest to the parched nature of the area.

and baking hot (up to 134°F or 56.7°C) (see page 163 for more information on rain shadows). Flights into Southern California usually fly over this area; watch for high mountains bordering a long, flat valley with a white pan at the bottom.

Until ten thousand years ago, conditions were very different in the Great Basin. At that time—the end of the latest Ice Age—freshwater seas covered the region. The mountaintops were island chains supporting a lush landscape teeming with mammoths, horses, camels, and rhinoceroses.

The Great Salt Lake is the largest remnant of these seas. At one time, an immense body of water that geologists call Lake Bonneville filled the basin around the Great Salt Lake, including all of the perfectly flat, white Great Salt Lake Desert (it really is salt you're seeing). Lake Bonneville, about one-third the size of modern Lake Michigan, was 1,000 feet (300 m) deep (the current lake averages only 14 feet, or 4 m), and its ancient shoreline is visible on the hills around Salt Lake City.

Fifteen thousand years ago, Lake Bonneville breached its northern rim, unleashing an unimaginable torrent into the Snake River Plain. The surface of the lake fell 330 feet (100 m) in a matter of days, leaving behind flood channels exactly like those identified on Mars from similar catastrophic events.

The extreme conditions of the Great Basin are matched by the extreme human activities that take place here. From roaring across the salt flats in rocket cars to testing nuclear weapons, whatever it is you want to do, you can probably get away with it here. Nearly a thousand nuclear bombs were exploded between 1951 and 1992 just 65 miles (105 km) northwest of Las Vegas—look that way as you fly in and out of Vegas and you might be able to glimpse craters formed by underground tests in the flat lake beds.

The Mojave, Sonora, and Chihuahuan Deserts

The Mojave Desert in southeastern California, the Sonora Desert spreading through southern Arizona and the Mexican state of Sonora, and the Chihuahuan Desert in southern New Mexico, far western Texas, and the Mexican state of Chihuahua, are the northernmost extensions of the profound desert of northern Mexico. Hot and dry, these regions developed unique ecosystems of highly specialized plants and animals, including the Mojave's famous Joshua trees and the giant saguaro cacti of the Sonora. From the air, you may be able to see these huge plants as dark dots spread across the landscape in southeastern California and southern Arizona.

The Mojave, in particular, features areas of stereotypical desert, with banks of drifting sand dunes visible from the air. Also watch for perfectly round volcanic cinder cones in this area. This material is used to surface roads throughout the region, which is why they are the same reddish color as the landscape.

0 1km 1mi

Of the ten fastest-growing cities in the United States in the 1990s, four—Las Vegas, Phoenix, Yuma AZ, and Provo UT—are situated in these deserts (Las Vegas, boasting the greatest surge, grew by 83 percent during that decade). Among these booming cities, more than two million people were added to this limited ecosystem (see page 52 for more information about urban sprawl).

As you fly into any of these cities, watch for abrupt subdivisions right across the street from native desert. Chances are, those houses weren't there five years ago, or even last year.

While human habitation may be sparse, our impact is not, and, because of the lack of rainfall and vegetation, human impact lasts a long, long time. In the Mojave, tank tracks left by General George Patton's Third Army as it trained in preparation for World War II are visible from the air outside Palm Springs: Look for hundreds of parallel lines running in all directions through the desert. In northern Nevada and eastern Oregon, the old wagon ruts of the Oregon Trail and other pioneer routes are still visible 150 years later. The subdivisions, highways, strip mines, and bomb craters we've put here in the intervening years will be with us for some time indeed.

FEDERAL LAND

Throughout the western United States, the federal government directly administers hundreds of millions of acres, which includes both the most sublime and rare landscapes and some of the most abominably polluted and ill-used areas in the world. The majority is administered by the U.S. Bureau of Land Management (BLM), whose 262 million acres (106 million hectares, or ha) amount to an eighth of the entire country, some of it in very large parcels: The contiguous area of BLM districts in eastern Oregon, for example, is larger than Massachusetts.

BLM land is often indicated by the presence of mines, which look like a factory on a rail line or road in the middle of nowhere next to a large pond or a small mountain of tailings; strip or open-pit mines look like large, stepped gouges in the planet's surface (see the photo on page 109). On BLM lands you also may be able to spot erosion as a result of overgrazing.

The U.S. Forest Service administers another 192 million acres (78 million ha)—about the size of Texas—and promotes economic use of these lands through forestry, hunting, and tourism. This land is usually forested and contains irregular patches of clearcuts (see the photos on pages 99 and 100).

Though its holdings are smaller—83 million acres (34 million ha)—the U.S. National Park Service lands attract more than 400 million visits each year from Alcatraz to Zion. Watch for spectacular natural features served by roads, and parking lots in remote places.

The U.S. Bureau of Indian Affairs (BIA) administers 56 million acres (23 million ha) in trust for the 1.2 million indigenous members of the 562 tribal nations in the United States. A legacy of one of the most shameful chapters in the country's history, the BIA—today 90 percent staffed by Native Americans—is now a development agency charged with the welfare of the poorest, least-developed parts of the country.

Military lands comprise 30 million acres (12 million ha) throughout the country, including the U.S. Army's White Sands Missile Range in New Mexico, which, at 3.6 million acres (1.5 million ha), is the largest single military property in the nation. The site of the first atomic-bomb blast ever, in 1945, this distinctive bright white mark on the landscape can often be seen from the air. Elsewhere, look for large but isolated airfields, mysteriously large buildings, regular groups of structures, and pockmarked bombing ranges.

The federal presence is so large in some areas—83 percent of the state of Nevada, for example, consists of federal land (and some counties are virtually entirely U.S. property)—that residents often feel as though federal personnel are colonial occupiers carrying out land-use decisions made far away in Washington, D.C. Federal agencies are often criticized for making unwise use of the land; BLM mining permits, for example, are notorious for returning very little to the national treasury while leaving atrocious messes behind.

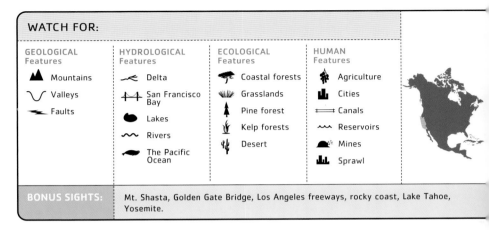

WATCH FOR:

GEOLOGICAL Features	HYDROLOGICAL Features	ECOLOGICAL Features	HUMAN Features
▲▲ Mountains	◅ Delta	🌲 Coastal forests	🌳 Agriculture
∨∫ Valleys	⊬⊢ San Francisco Bay	🌾 Grasslands	�🏛 Cities
➤ Faults	● Lakes	🌲 Pine forest	⊨ Canals
	∼∼ Rivers	🌿 Kelp forests	∿∿∿ Reservoirs
	➤ The Pacific Ocean	🌵 Desert	⛰ Mines
			�📊 Sprawl

BONUS SIGHTS: Mt. Shasta, Golden Gate Bridge, Los Angeles freeways, rocky coast, Lake Tahoe, Yosemite.

Ever since Europeans first arrived on its pleasant coast, California has evoked an aura of paradise. This is a golden promised land, the place where America (and much of the world) comes to create the future. It is the most populated state (almost 35 million people, about one-eighth of the country's population, live here), and, were it an independent country, its economy would be the fifth largest in the world (between the United Kingdom and France).

From the air, California offers a gorgeous collection of vistas. If you fly to California from the east during the winter, the first thing you'll notice is how green it is. After 2,000 miles (3,200 km) of dun drabness, the emerald carpet below is refreshing and uplifting. Conversely, if you arrive during the summer, the state's golden glow seems buffed to an improbably rich sheen.

Physically, California is composed of two long mountain ranges interspersed with several sets of basins, all running northwest to southeast. The basic functional mechanism for this landscape's formation (and the source of California's famous earthquakes) is the tectonic collision of the Pacific Plate with the North American Plate (see page 32 for more information about plate tectonics).

The Sierra Nevada mountains, in the east of the state, were formed by vast gobs of molten rock—melted pieces of the Pacific Plate—rising sixty million years ago into the continental plate above. It's easy to

0 1 km 1 mi

SAN FRANCISCO BAY ➤
The San Francisco Bay
Area is a sublime place for
human habitation, featuring
a sheltered anchorage, mild
climate, bountiful agricultural areas, access to the
interior (the Golden Gate
1 is the only break in the
Coast Range), and plentiful
raw materials like wood
and water. Now, however, a
century and a half after
settlement began, the
presence of almost 8 million
people has heavily altered
the bay, one-third of which
has been filled in. The

flows of the Sacramento
and San Joaquin Rivers
through the system have
been drastically reduced,
allowing saltwater intru-
sion into the bay and delta.
The bay itself has been
polluted, too, and the basin
around it routinely fills
with smog. Nonetheless,
this is still a fine place to
live, and in recent decades
steps have been taken to
clean things up.
     Other features of note
in this image include San
Francisco itself **2** and a
number of seismic faults,

particularly visible in the
Oakland Hills **3**. Just outside this image are Silicon
Valley to the south and
Napa to the north. Napa is
both a world-renowned
wine-growing region and a
top tourist destination—
one of the few places you
will see agriculture along-
side hallmarks of affluence
like golf courses, swimming
pools, and mansions. But,
like the Bay Area as whole,
the balance is delicate: Too
much development would
eliminate the reason people
are drawn to the area.

imagine this batholith rising as you look down on the smooth, bare granite lobes scattered throughout the range.

Even after eons of erosion and glaciation, the Sierra Nevada remains a long, foreboding wall of granite that includes the highest peak in the conterminous United States: Mount Whitney, at 14,494 feet (4,418 m). In spite of its great height, you'll be able to spot Mount Whitney only if you know exactly where to look, as many other high peaks surround it— look for a high wall of mountains at the southern end of the Sierra

PALM SPRINGS, CALIFORNIA ⊱ After you cross the hard browns of the desert, catching sight of the golf oasis of Palm Springs in the Mojave Desert, east of Los Angeles, is always startling. As with all development in the desert, Palm Springs is utterly dependent on water brought in from elsewhere. Here and in the lush agri- cultural areas of the Imperial Valley to the south, the dividing line between irrigated and unirrigated land is razor sharp, highlighting the effort it takes to maintain this landscape.

INSTITUTIONS

The campus landscape—a collection of buildings arranged in a parklike setting—has become typical of large institutions in North America. This design is in part derived from Oxford University, the model for many of the oldest universities in both the United States and Canada. It has since been adopted by many kinds of institutions that must integrate a wide variety of activities—from offices to recreation to dining—in a small area.

Some examples you are likely to see on your flight include universities, prisons, hospitals, military bases, and corporate campuses. Each installation has its own distinctive characteristics, with prison features being perhaps the most extreme: Perimeters clear of buildings and shrubbery, fences (often in pairs, which you might be able to spot if you're not at cruising altitude), and architecture designed to permit clear views by guards (sharp angles, H-shaped buildings, and other configurations). At night, prisons are brightly illuminated and, because they are often in rural areas, they can be spotted very easily.

The U.S. Federal Penitentiary outside Lompoc, California, displays all these features. The high-security prison, housing 1,500 inmates and employing 500 guards, is surrounded by open fields and hills.

In contrast, the University of Colorado at Boulder is open to the city around it. The university accommodates more than 30,000 staff and students. The stadium is a telltale sign of a university campus, as are the sweeping networks of pedestrian walkways that connect the buildings.

Unlike many of our public spaces, campuses are explicitly designed for walking—note the very limited parking around the Folsom Stadium here, and compare it with professional sports stadiums, which usually float in a sea of parking places (see, for example, Dodger Stadium in the photo on page 120).

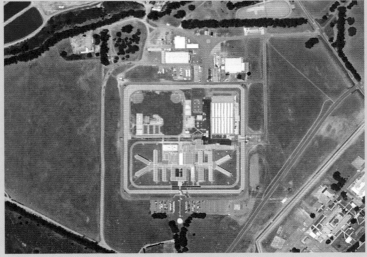

U.S. Federal Penitentiary

University of Colorado

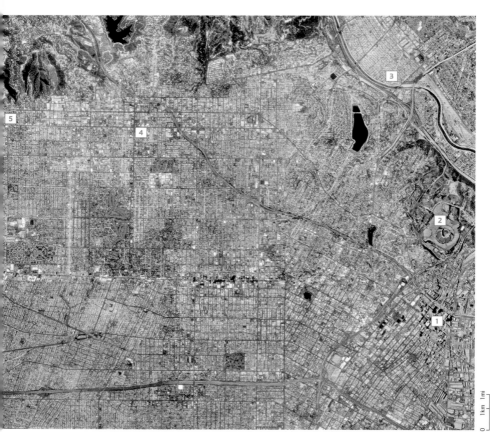

LOS ANGELES ➤ Ten million people live in Los Angeles County, making this the most populous city in the United States. It has sprawled through several originally distinct communities (now chiefly evident from the varying orientations of their street grids) to cover the Southern Californian coastal plain with an undifferentiated film of strip malls, housing, warehouses, and business districts. This image includes downtown Los Angeles **1**, Dodger Stadium **2**, several interstates, the Los Angeles River **3**, and dozens of mixed residential neighborhoods, including Hollywood **4** and Beverly Hills **5**.

As the car and the American idea of the middle-class suburb has spread around the world, Los Angeles has replaced New York and the European capitals as the model for modern urbanism. But residents are caught in a bind: The convenience of driving has become a necessity, and commutes of 100 miles or more are not uncommon. As a result, the exhaust of the 9 million motor vehicles here often becomes trapped by the mountains that flank the city, generating a soupy brown smog that, as you fly into any airport in the region, looks like a layered lake of smoke (see page 165 for more information on smog).

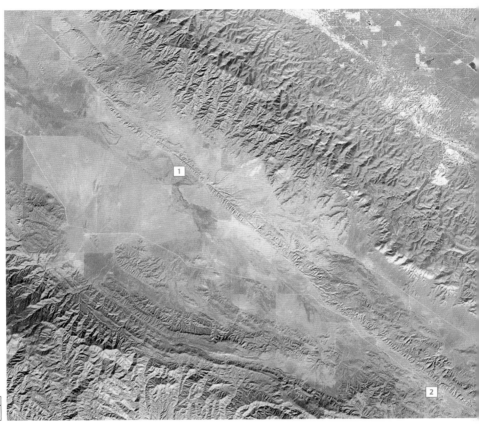

0 1 km 1 mi

THE SAN ANDREAS FAULT ⊱ The San Andreas Fault, the suture between the North American Plate to the east, and the Pacific Plate to the west, stretches from Baja California to just north of San Francisco, and is 6 miles (10 km) or more deep (see page 32 for more information about tectonic plates). Seen here, about halfway between San Francisco and Los Angeles, the fault is a long, straight valley **1** that contains river courses **2** bent by the northward movement of the plate on the western side of the fault. The San Andreas fault system is responsible for the most destructive earthquakes in the region. Once you spot it you'll see, nonetheless, considerable development along its length, including roads, dams, canals, and reservoirs.

Nevada, snow-covered in winter and spring, rising sharply above the final basin of the Basin and Range. Whitney is the tallest of these peaks. The flight between San Francisco and Las Vegas should give you the best chance to spot it.

0 1km 1mi

YOSEMITE ➤ Yosemite National Park is a particularly spectacular part of the Sierra Nevada batholith, where the exposed granite lobes bubbled up from melted chunks of the subducted Pacific Plate. The often smooth, polished surface of the rock, as well as the broad shape of the valleys, is due to repeated glaciation over the past one million years. The forest here is primarily pine, dense in the sheltered valleys and sparse or absent on higher, exposed rock areas.

Yosemite is one of the nation's leading tourist attractions, with more than 4 million visitors each year. This influx, however, greatly impacts the valley, which is sometimes obscured by a haze of smog.

Flights between San Francisco and southwest destinations like Las Vegas and Phoenix frequently pass right over Yosemite. On a clear day from this vantage point, you can see the Pacific Ocean, the Coast Range, the Central Valley, the Sierra Nevada, Mount Whitney, Death Valley, Mono Lake, and the Mojave Desert all at once.

The subduction of the Pacific Plate also gave rise to the Coast Range. As the Pacific Plate moved under the North American Plate over the past one hundred million years, chunks of lighter rock, pieces of continental and oceanic crust, and island arcs on the top of the plate plowed into the shore. Because these pieces of rock (called exotic

135

THE GREAT CENTRAL
VALLEY ➤ The towns of
Ripon **1** and Salida **2** hug
Highway 99 in the San
Joaquin Valley, the southern half of the Great Central
Valley. The San Joaquin
River **3** meanders at the
bottom left of this image,
surrounded by the sort of
riparian floodplain forest
that once filled much of
the valley. One of the most

productive agricultural
regions on Earth, the valley
is farmed intensively by
large agribusiness corpora-
tions to produce tomatoes,
lettuce, rice, various fruits,
and many other crops, but
this land is also in high
demand for development,
and a nearly continuous
urban and suburban corri-
dor is forming from the
San Francisco Bay Area to

Sacramento and south to
Bakersfield. While it is still
the leading agricultural
state, 20,000 acres (8,100
ha) of California farmland
are developed each year—
the San Joaquin Valley
has lost one-tenth of its
farmland since 1982 and
is expected to lose one-
fifth by 2010 (see page
52 for more information
about urban sprawl).

PUNTA GORDA ➤ Punta Gorda is part of the Mendocino fracture zone, a very seismically active area of the Northern California coast where a set of large faults (including the San Andreas, which is just offshore here) head out to sea. The Mattole River  runs along one of these faults and is the epicenter of hundreds of quakes each year. Twelve miles (20 km) beneath this coast, the oceanic mantle of the Pacific Plate is sliding under the North American Plate, where it melts in the great heat of Earth's interior.

As you travel north, the forest becomes more and more dense due to the increasing rainfall, but it is still interspersed here with grassland—golden in the rainless summer months—on the hotter and drier south-facing hillsides. The coastal forest is mirrored by the kelp forests—the blobs you can see just off the rocky coastline **2**. This complex marine environment of tall kelp strands teems with fish, seals, otters, sharks, and more.

terranes) have come from all over the Pacific, the Coast Range is stupendously varied.

Between the Sierra Nevada and the Coast Range lies the Great Central Valley, a perfectly flat area of rich cropland. Formerly a sea, the

Central Valley filled with first volcanic and then alluvial deposits over the past 135 million years to a depth of 30,000 feet (9,100 m)—just a little less than the cruising altitude of your plane!

To the north of the Central Valley, the Coast Range and the Cascades come together in the rugged Klamath Knot. Here, and in the Mojave Desert to the east of Los Angeles, you'll see how quickly the populated areas of the West give way to profound wilderness. Nonetheless, the populated areas are growing. Each year, California adds more than a million people to its population of 35 million, and you'll see the effects of this growth throughout the state. In particular, look for new suburbs replacing farmland in the Central Valley and the San Francisco Bay Area, and desert in the southland outside Los Angeles. Nearly everywhere there is a thriving city, you will see the unmistakable serpentine roads of new subdivisions.

This growth is coming at great environmental cost. Not only are rare habitats being lost, but some of the nation's best farmland is now producing ranch houses instead of vegetables. Worse, growth is imposing new demands on the limited water supply here, creating political tension. Within the state, water issues are a perennial sore point between relatively moist Northern California and arid Southern California. Throughout the West, thirsty California is frequently at odds with the even more rapidly growing desert states.

Still, California has such an inviting climate, beautiful landscape, and welcoming culture that, though it is the most populous state in the nation, it continues to attract people from around the country and around the world. It remains to be seen how long this golden land will remain so attractive in the face of this transformation.

CANADA CANADA CANADA

CANADA CANADA CA

CANADA CANADA

High Arctic

Arctic Ocean

Tundra

Western
Cordillera

Tundra

Tundra

Hudson Bay

CANADA

Pacific
Coast

Vancouver

Prairies

Canadian Shield
& Taiga

Saint Lawrence Seaway

Maritime

Montreal

Southern
Ontario

Toronto

USA

Pacific Ocean

Atlantic Ocean

MEXICO

Gulf of Mexico

CANADA

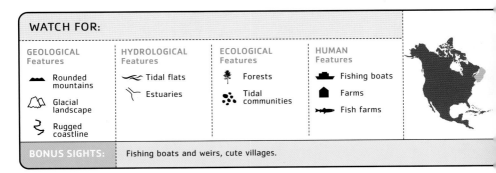

WATCH FOR:

GEOLOGICAL Features	HYDROLOGICAL Features	ECOLOGICAL Features	HUMAN Features
Rounded mountains	Tidal flats	Forests	Fishing boats
Glacial landscape	Estuaries	Tidal communities	Farms
Rugged coastline			Fish farms

BONUS SIGHTS: Fishing boats and weirs, cute villages.

Canada's Maritime Provinces—Nova Scotia, New Brunswick, Prince Edward Island (PEI), and Newfoundland—are actually the northern limb of the Appalachians (see page 44 for more information about the Appalachians). Here, the range descends into the ocean, and the coastline is a rugged combination of hard rock and cold water, with thousands of coves, inlets, and fjords (glacial valleys flooded by the ocean). From the air, this rough coast gives some hint of the challenges faced by people who settled here and those who live here today.

The Bay of Fundy, between Nova Scotia and New Brunswick, has the highest tides in the world and supports a unique and very productive marine ecosystem. From the air, you may be able to spot the extensive flats or seaweed-covered rocks exposed during low tide, when the water falls as far as 16 meters (53 ft) from the high-tide mark of just six hours previously. In the process, 100 billion tons of water flows in and out of the bay.

The economy here depends on the sea, but has stagnated for decades due to overfishing. One bright spot (economically, if not ecologically) is the fish farming you will see along the coast. These floating pens—rectangular, enclosed docks floating just offshore in sheltered areas—house millions of farmed Atlantic salmon.

Inland, a patchwork of bucolic farms spreads across the land. PEI's landscape is almost entirely farmland (potatoes grow particularly well in its heavy red soil), while the interiors of New Brunswick and Newfoundland are much more rugged and wild, and are covered in evergreen forest.

THE BAY OF FUNDY ➤
The Petitcodiac and
Membramcook Rivers
enter the Bay of Fundy
at its head in New
Brunswick. French long

lots **1** (see page 74) define
the settlement patterns
along both waterways.
Inland, the small towns
and woodlots are typical
of the Maritime Provinces.

The bay's extreme tides
create a dynamic shoreline:
The wide mud flat **2** will
be completely submerged
when the tide rises.

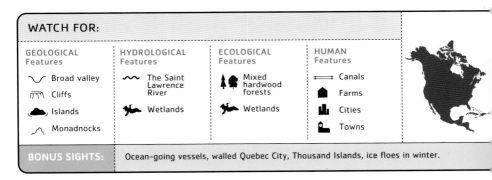

WATCH FOR:

GEOLOGICAL Features	HYDROLOGICAL Features	ECOLOGICAL Features	HUMAN Features
Broad valley	The Saint Lawrence River	Mixed hardwood forests	Canals
Cliffs	Wetlands	Wetlands	Farms
Islands			Cities
Monadnocks			Towns

BONUS SIGHTS: Ocean-going vessels, walled Quebec City, Thousand Islands, ice floes in winter.

The Saint Lawrence drains the Great Lakes and is the last leg of one of the largest freshwater systems in the world. It is also the gateway to the heart of the continent for oceangoing vessels, except in the winter, when ice blocks this huge river (see page 61 for more information about the Great Lakes). In the warmer months you'll see large freighters working their way through the system, some going as far as Thunder Bay, Ontario, and Duluth, Minnesota, where they will load the bounteous grains of the middle of the continent for shipment around the world.

Though huge—at its mouth it is 145 kilometers (90 mi.) wide—the Saint Lawrence River is very young. It began to follow its present course along a very old and deep fault only ten thousand years ago, when the glaciers of the latest Ice Age retreated far enough north.

High above the river, on the site of an indigenous Huron village, Quebec City is the oldest European settlement on the Saint Lawrence. Established by France in 1608 as a fur-trading outpost, Quebec City eventually became the seat of French power in the north. From the air, you will see the old walled city—the only one in North America outside Mexico. Watch for the telltale narrow streets surrounding the green-roofed Chateau Frontenac—a stately old hotel that looks like a castle. On the Plains of Abraham, outside the city and above the river, British forces defeated the French in 1759, establishing British dominance of North America.

THE SAINT LAWRENCE RIVER ➤ The Eastern Townships lie to the east and south of the Saint Lawrence River **1** outside Montreal. Though the region was settled by English-speaking Loyalists to the British Crown who had fled the American Revolution, the land is laid out in French long lots. The smaller Richelieu River **2** flows north from Lake Champlain in Vermont to join the region's primary waterway. Mont–Saint–Hilaire **3**, near the town of Beloeil, is a monadnock— a blob of solid basement rock that has extended upward into softer layers that later eroded around it. The picturesque towns here are in commuting distance to Montreal, just to the southwest of this image, and you can see them sprawl into one another as a result.

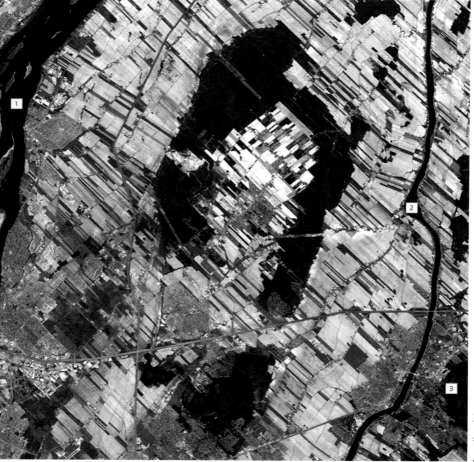

1 km 1 mi

0

THE THOUSAND ISLANDS
➤ The town of Gananoque, Ontario **1**, is the gateway to the Thousand Islands— a rocky archipelago where the Saint Lawrence River crosses the Canadian Shield

and leaves Lake Ontario. At the transition between Upper and Lower Canada, this area has both French long lots **2** (see page 74) and British square lots **3** settled by Loyalists. The

pinkish area near the Gananoque River **4** is part of the extensive marshlands you will see in Southern Ontario. The border between the U.S. and Canada winds among these islands.

Montreal is the second-largest city in Canada. Its three and a half million inhabitants live on an island in the Saint Lawrence River at the highest natural point of navigation. Farther upriver, where the Saint Lawrence flows out of Lake Ontario, the river marks the border between Canada and the United States. Here, you'll find the Thousand Islands, and from the air you can see why they're so named. These islands, a chaotic jumble of glacial features and rock outcroppings, form a geological link between the Adirondacks to the south and the Canadian Shield to the north. In addition to the eponymous salad dressing, this area is known for its watery recreational opportunities.

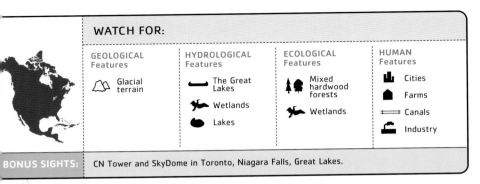

WATCH FOR:

GEOLOGICAL Features	HYDROLOGICAL Features	ECOLOGICAL Features	HUMAN Features
Glacial terrain	The Great Lakes	Mixed hardwood forests	Cities
	Wetlands	Wetlands	Farms
	Lakes		Canals
			Industry

BONUS SIGHTS: CN Tower and SkyDome in Toronto, Niagara Falls, Great Lakes.

Bustling with cities and industry, this region of Canada is home to a fifth of all Canadians. Geologically, Southern Ontario is a part of the Great Lakes and the Midwest, sharing the sandy, glacial geological characteristics of Michigan, Indiana, and Ohio (see page 66 for more information about glaciers). It also shares the same weather (including tornadoes) and crops (particularly corn), but its overall landscape is distinctive, with many small farms and towns. Like its neighbors in the Midwest, Southern Ontario is also the manufacturing heartland of its nation.

Because of the moderating influence of the Great Lakes, which surround Southern Ontario, the region's climate is far more benign than its latitude and location in the interior of the continent would otherwise suggest. As a result, rich farmland here produces crops that are otherwise difficult or impossible to grow in Canada. The area to the south of Lake Ontario, for example, is known for its fruits and wines—delicacies largely unknown outside British Columbia.

Toronto dominates this region. The largest city in Canada, Toronto is a dynamic metropolis on the shores of Lake Ontario. From the air, you can see it sprawl away from the downtown center and northward from the lake (see page 52 for more information about urban sprawl).

Carved out of a profound wilderness to be the capital of Upper Canada just two hundred years ago, the city has changed dramatically from its days as a wilderness outpost of the British Empire. The woods, once so tall and thick as to evoke a helpless melancholy in settlers, have given way to a modern sprawl of concrete and development.

NIAGARA FALLS ➤ The Niagara River **1** separates the cities of Niagara Falls, Ontario, on the left, and Niagara Falls, New York, on the right. The massive falls **2** where the river narrows into the Niagara Gorge before spilling into Lake Ontario **3** are a world-famous tourist attraction, as well as the source of one-quarter of the electricity used in Ontario and New York state, thanks to the hydro-electric generating stations here **4** . This is the busiest part of the border between the two nations, with 14 million people crossing each year—40 percent of all land traffic between the two countries. The Welland Canal **5** , part of the Saint Lawrence Seaway, bypasses the falls and allows oceangoing vessels to move higher into the Great Lakes.

TORONTO ⊱ The low glacial till of Southern Ontario offers little impediment to the sprawl of Canada's largest city. Located on the north shore of Lake Ontario, Toronto has long been the cultural and economic center of English-speaking Canada. In this image, you can see counties laid out along different axes. The rivers and ravines that branch throughout the city (treed areas) flow in parallel grooves left behind by an ice lobe centered over Lake Ontario more than ten thousand years ago. The same lobe also created the Oak Ridges Moraine— a long ridge you might spot north of the city.

Toronto has become uniquely multicultural and cosmopolitan, with a relatively harmonious blend of peoples from all over the world. It is renowned for its civility and safety in spite of—or perhaps because of— its extreme diversity. Toronto is the financial, cultural, and political center of English-speaking Canada. With five million people, 17 percent of the nation, the influence of this city is felt throughout the country.

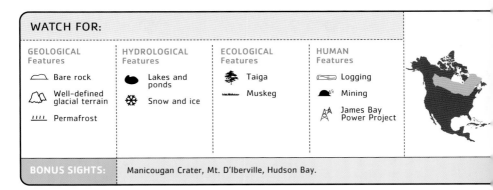

WATCH FOR:

GEOLOGICAL Features	HYDROLOGICAL Features	ECOLOGICAL Features	HUMAN Features
Bare rock	Lakes and ponds	Taiga	Logging
Well-defined glacial terrain	Snow and ice	Muskeg	Mining
Permafrost			James Bay Power Project

BONUS SIGHTS: Manicougan Crater, Mt. D'Iberville, Hudson Bay.

The inhabitants of the Canadian Shield and the taiga are still predominantly indigenous. While the majority live in towns and many participate in the modern regional economy of mining and logging, others still travel deep into the bush to hunt and fish in the tradition of their ancestors. Hundreds of thousands here speak Algonquian and Athabaskan indigenous languages.

The Canadian Shield, an enormous chunk of ancient rock that forms the granite heart of North America, covers almost two-thirds of Canada in an immense crescent around Hudson Bay.

This hard gray granite formed when the liquid magma that made up the planet at its birth (and that fills Earth's interior today) cooled. Nearly three billion years old, the Canadian Shield includes some of the oldest rock known (Earth itself is four and a half billion years old, and the oldest known evidence of life is from three billion years ago).

If you are flying over Quebec, watch for the perfectly circular Manicougan crater, product of a meteorite impact more than two hundred million years ago that now forms an unmistakable ring-shaped reservoir 100 kilometers (60 mi.) across. Since the solid rock of the Canadian Shield is impermeable to water, tens of thousands of lakes have formed in this enormous, undulating rock garden. From the air, it often seems to be more water than land—not surprising, since Canada contains one-quarter of the world's freshwater. Some of the largest bodies

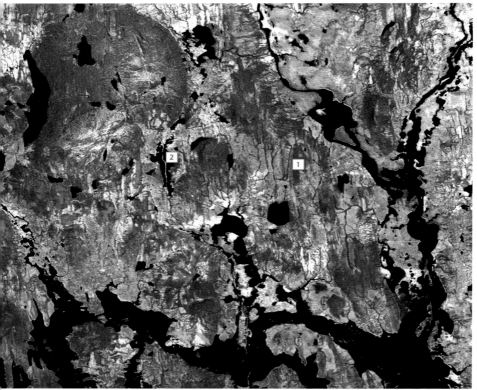

A GLACIAL LANDSCAPE ➤ The rocky uplands of southern Quebec are covered in drumlins (elongated hills **1**), eskers (sinuous ridges—note the esker that parts the small lake **2**), water-filled depressions, and scour marks. The orientation of these features, and of the rivers in the area (once glacial spillways), shows the direction of movement of the ice sheet that covered this region 10,000 years ago. This landscape is typical of the Canadian Shield, with areas of bare rock, taiga (boreal forest), lakes everywhere, marshy wetlands, and late spring snow.

of water here are the reservoirs of the James Bay Power Project strung across northern Quebec into Labrador.

The Taiga

Because this region is so immense, its surface features change considerably with latitude. In the south, covering much of Saskatchewan, Manitoba, Ontario, and Quebec, lies an immense swath of evergreen forest called the taiga, or boreal forest. This kind of forested terrain circles the globe in Canada, Alaska, Russia, and Scandinavia. (*Taiga* is a central Asian word for this kind of forest in Siberia.) Because of the difficult climate, the taiga is a relatively stunted and sparse forest.

In addition to long, icy winters, waterlogged and thin soils, and a short growing season, the taiga is subject to frequent forest fires, creating a patchwork you can see from the air. The taiga is also an important paper-producing region: Look for large paper mills near bodies of water. There are often trucks lined up outside them, filled with chipped trees. You'll notice many large clearcuts where the forest has been removed. These generally have geometrical shapes and clean edges, while clearings due to fire are ragged and, if recent, blackened. In the winter, clearings of all kinds stand out as white, snowy patches in the dark forest. While they may look similar to frozen lakes, bodies of water are more rounded.

Hudson Bay

During the latest Ice Age, Hudson Bay was covered by several giant ice caps 3 to 5 kilometers (2 to 3 mi.) thick, similar to the one in Greenland today. The weight of this ice deformed the Canadian Shield enough to leave a basin filled with seawater when the ice melted. This basin is still rebounding; the shore of Hudson Bay recedes by 1 meter (3 ft.) a year as a result. The latest glaciation here was very recent: The last ice finally broke up five thousand years ago, when the Great Pyramids were being built in Egypt (see page 66 for more information about glaciers).

The flat area along the bay's southern shore, a region of sedimentary rocks atop the Canadian Shield, is a seemingly endless swamp of muskeg—subarctic peat swamp. You'll see that it's absolutely flat and sparkles with small bodies of water everywhere (except in winter, of course, when the water is frozen and snow covered). From here northward, the climate is cool enough that ice can remain in the soil all year long—solid water thus becomes a geological element called permafrost.

Along the Edges

At the eastern edge of the Canadian Shield in Quebec and Labrador, the Torngat Mountains rise to 1,646 meters (5,400 ft.) at Mount d'Iberville, making them the highest peaks in the eastern half of North America. Because of the nearby ocean, these heavily eroded and glaciated mountains

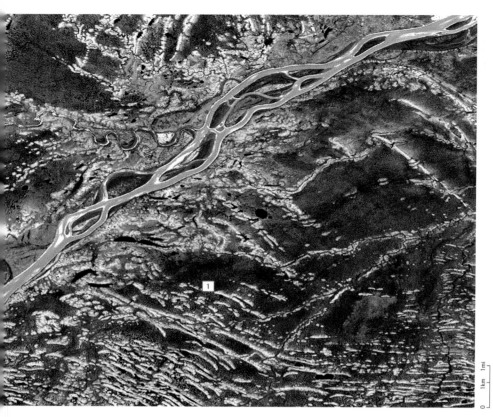

THE HUDSON BAY
LOWLANDS ≻ Muskeg—
cool, sodden peatland—
extends south from Hudson
Bay. The ridges **1** are old

shorelines of the rapidly
receding bay. A little higher
than the wetlands around
them, these ridges often
support shrubs and some-

times trees. They cover
pockets of permafrost
(permanently frozen
ground) just a meter or so
(a few feet) beneath them.

receive more precipitation than the rest of the Canadian Shield.
Nonetheless, they are frigid and can support vegetation only in the
most sheltered areas.

Along the western edge of the Canadian Shield lies a chain of huge
lakes, remnants of even larger glacial bodies of water. From south to
north, these include the Great Lakes, Lake Winnipeg, Lake Athabaska,
Great Slave Lake, and Great Bear Lake. To the west of the Canadian
Shield, the taiga spreads out across flat plains of sedimentary rock and
permafrost. This region is centered on the Mackenzie River, the second

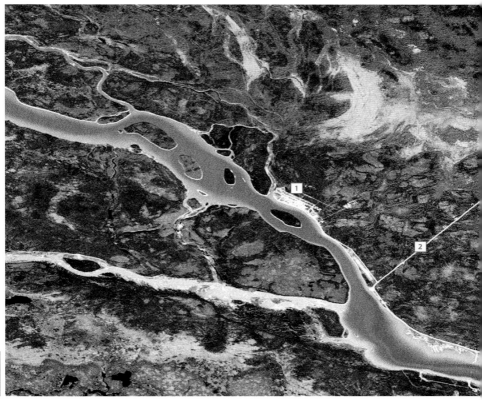

THE MACKENZIE RIVER ⟩ The town of Fort Providence **1** (population 837) hugs the shore of the Mackenzie River shortly after it leaves Great Slave Lake in the Northwest Territories. The town's streets and the road leading north **2** to Yellowknife are white with snow; in the winter, the river freezes and a more direct ice road is established on its surface. From here, the huge, wild river (the tenth largest in the world) flows almost 2,000 km (1,240 miles) to the Arctic Ocean, meandering and braiding without a single bridge over it.

largest on the continent (after the Mississippi). The area was free of Ice Age glaciers much earlier than regions to the east and west, and formed a corridor for the settlement of the Americas by people moving across a land bridge connecting North America to Asia.

THE PRAIRIES

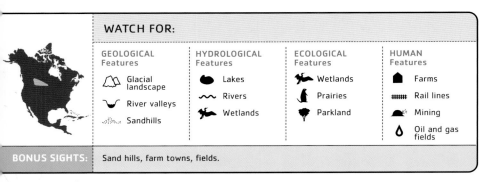

WATCH FOR:

GEOLOGICAL Features	HYDROLOGICAL Features	ECOLOGICAL Features	HUMAN Features
Glacial landscape	Lakes	Wetlands	Farms
River valleys	Rivers	Prairies	Rail lines
Sandhills	Wetlands	Parkland	Mining
			Oil and gas fields

The Canadian Prairies are Canada's breadbasket, producing wheat and canola for the whole world. They are the northern limb of the High Plains grasslands that fill the center of the North American continent from Texas to Alberta. Their geological and ecological history is similar to that of the High Plains to the south, but toward the north, with wetter conditions, is a transition zone of aspen parkland, where steppe grasslands and taiga trees intermingle.

Even more than the Great Plains, the Canadian Prairies are heavily altered, with more than 95 percent of the land now used for farming and grazing. From the air, you will see neat communities separated by the gigantic farms that make this one of the world's major wheat- and canola-growing regions.

You'll also see the effects of the two major forces that have shaped this landscape: water and ice. The Prairies were molded by the ice sheets of the latest glaciation, which left moraines, drumlins, eskers, and kettle ponds (see page 66 for definitions of glaciation terms) on this broad outwash plain. Flowing glacial meltwater and modern rivers have carved valleys into this plain that form a drainage network flowing out of the Rockies to the west. The wetlands fed by these waters are very important habitat: Half of all North American ducks are born here. See if you can spot the dense flocks—dark blobs against the water below.

For a century, up until 1870, all the land that drained into Hudson Bay, including the Prairies, belonged to the Hudson Bay Company under charter from the British Crown. Unfortunately, the company overharvested fur-bearing animals here and contributed greatly to the

SASKATOON, SASKATCHEWAN
> Surrounded by the
rich farmland of central
Saskatchewan, Saskatoon
is a regional center of
more than 200,000 inhabi-
tants. Along the South
Saskatchewan River, the
city was first established
as a temperance colony in
the 1880s and quickly
grew under an influx of

immigrants more interested
in opportunity than absti-
nence. In this image, you
can see the numerous
transportation links—rail,
road, water, and air—that
make Saskatoon the central
city of the region. Unlike
parts of Canada farther
east, the land here is laid
out according to the western survey system, an

orderly grid applied to
Saskatchewan in the 1880s
(although the northern
parts of the province were
not surveyed until the
1960s). Saskatoon is not
far from the northern limit
of farmable land, after
which aspen parkland and
taiga take over.

near extinction of the once-abundant bison. In 1870, Canada bought the
land, and settlement began in an effort to thwart the territorial ambi-
tions of the United States. Settlers came largely from the overcrowded
rural areas of Eastern Europe. Finally able to own land, these industri-
ous old-world farmers were responsible for transforming the native
prairie into the rich agricultural landscape you see below you.

SAND HILLS ≻ Sand hills like this can be found in pockets across the Great Plains of the United States and the Canadian Prairies, with the largest concentrations in southwestern Saskatchewan and western Nebraska. These unfarmable areas—they are used for grazing instead—feature drifting sand dunes **1** and a unique grassland ecology. The farms surrounding them are strip-cropped **2** with wheat, canola, and other crops as a measure against wind erosion—a battle some are clearly losing. A few natural gas wells are visible in this image as white cleared areas with dirt roads leading to them **3**.

0   1km   1mi

THE WESTERN CORDILLERA

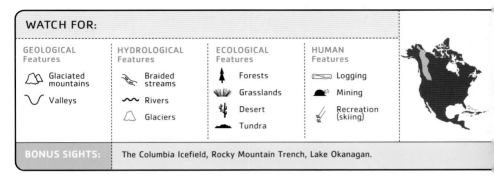

WATCH FOR:

GEOLOGICAL Features	HYDROLOGICAL Features	ECOLOGICAL Features	HUMAN Features
Glaciated mountains	Braided streams	Forests	Logging
Valleys	Rivers	Grasslands	Mining
	Glaciers	Desert	Recreation (skiing)
		Tundra	

BONUS SIGHTS: The Columbia Icefield, Rocky Mountain Trench, Lake Okanagan.

The Western Cordillera comprises the western ramparts of Canada. Its ranges include the Columbia Mountains and the Canadian Rockies— part of the same range found to the south, in the western United States. The stunning mountains of the Western Cordillera present an unbroken vista of sharp peaks, stark snowfields, and dense forests. The small human population here is spread out in the narrow valleys—many communities are very isolated. People here live very close to the land, working as loggers or farmers or depending on the steady flow of visitors to this magnificent wilderness.

Formed by uplift from the collision of the North American Plate with the plates under the Pacific, these lofty peaks were carved by heavy glaciation into the cirques and arêtes you see today (see page 66 for information about glaciation and page 32 for information about plate tectonics). As you fly overhead, you'll even see a few living glaciers, remnants of the latest Ice Age; the Columbia Icefield, on the border between Alberta and British Columbia, is the largest you'll see this far south in North America. An ice dome more than 300 meters (1,000 ft.) thick, it's located at a hydrographic apex: Its waters flow to the Pacific Ocean, the Arctic Ocean, and Hudson Bay.

As in the south, the Rockies rise up suddenly from the prairies, but here they form a near-solid mountainous region that extends all the way to the coast, covering most of British Columbia and the Yukon. These mountains are heavily forested at lower elevations, and you will see evidence of much logging. The valleys, particularly in the south, are rich agricultural lands that produce some of Canada's finest fruit crops.

The Okanagan Valley, for example, is known for its orchards and vineyards. In summer, watch for the green rows of grapevines on the valley bottom (if you're flying over at just the right time in the fall, they'll be a patchwork of bright yellow and red). The valley's pleasant climate and scenic beauty draw thousands of tourists each year, further enhancing its standing as a pillar of the regional economy.

To the north, in the Klondike and beyond, the Western Cordillera becomes more and more wild and remote, eventually becoming arctic and barren on the ice-scoured shores of the Beaufort Sea. This region showcases a spectacular mountain wilderness, with some of the highest peaks, biggest waterfalls, wildest rivers, and deepest canyons in Canada.

THE COLUMBIA ICEFIELD ⊱ In Alberta, near Banff and Jasper and not far from Calgary, the Columbia Icefield straddles the Continental Divide. A remnant of the ice sheets that once covered all of Canada, it provides an excellent look at how glaciers form mountain landscapes. The glacial tongues **1**, flowing down from the icefield in U-shaped valleys, are surrounded by moraines, and you can spot arêtes **2** and cirques **3** being formed. Try to imagine glaciers like this on top of other mountains you may see, and it will help you understand how they came to look the way they do.

THE ROCKY MOUNTAIN TRENCH ≻ The Rocky Mountain Trench, a north–south system of faults extending nearly 1,600 km (1,000 miles) from Montana to the Yukon, divides the Rockies in the east from the older Colombia Mountains in the west. Watch for long, straight lines of huge mountains separated by a long, wide valley (the longest in North America). Every flight between the Pacific Coast and the rest of Canada crosses the trench, which is clearly visible from space. Kinbasket Reservoir, which peeks into this image at the lower right **1**, covers 216 km (134 miles) of the Columbia River's course through the trench. The town of Valemount **2** (incorporated in 1962) is in the middle of the trench and has an active tourism sector devoted to the spectacular mountains in the area. The patches on the slope southwest of town are clearcuts **3**, evidence of the other mainstay of the local economy.

This is a profound and largely unspoiled wilderness, one that only a few people are hardy and skilled enough to live in. The primordial mountains are as unforgiving as they are beautiful, and the comfort of a window seat is the closest most of us will ever get to this haunting land.

THE PACIFIC COAST

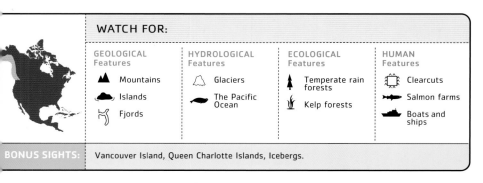

WATCH FOR:

GEOLOGICAL Features	HYDROLOGICAL Features	ECOLOGICAL Features	HUMAN Features
▲▲ Mountains	△ Glaciers	↑ Temperate rain forests	Clearcuts
Islands	The Pacific Ocean	Kelp forests	Salmon farms
Fjords			Boats and ships

BONUS SIGHTS: Vancouver Island, Queen Charlotte Islands, Icebergs.

Beginning near the border between the United States and Canada, from Puget Sound and Vancouver Island northward, the western coast of North America takes on a distinctive, complex character. Heavily glaciated in the past and very seismically active, this region is a riot of high mountains and deep fjords, making for some of the most spectacular scenery on the planet.

Like the shoreline farther south, the coast shared by British Columbia and Alaska is composed of huge pieces of Earth's crust that have rafted into the North American Plate.

Island arcs are still being pushed into the continent here, and you will see hundreds of them destined to join the mainland. For now, however, they serve to protect the Inside Passage—a calm waterway that makes for easy marine travel along the coast.

The region's great fjords—several reaching well over 100 kilometers (62 mi.) inland—are among the world's longest and deepest. The sheer walls, reaching up to 2 kilometers (1.2 mi.) tall, were formed by unrelenting glaciation during the latest Ice Age. Here, the glaciers came right to the ocean and calved great icebergs—a process you can still witness farther north along this coast.

The Pacific coast is home to some of the greatest temperate rain forests on the planet—the west side of Vancouver Island, for example, receives the most rainfall of any place in North America, and the temperature is relatively warm, making conditions ideal. The mountainsides are blanketed with deep green forests that stretch from the water's edge to the treeline.

0 1km 1mi

PACIFIC FJORDS ≻ The coast of British Columbia is a riot of fjords left behind by glaciers that once calved icebergs here. If you're flying north, you'll see this landscape being created in Alaska. The mountain-sides are blanketed in old-growth rain forest, though here and there you can see clearings due to avalanche, rockfall, and clearcut logging.

In these forests, you will see two kinds of catastrophic clearing, one natural and the other by the hand of humankind. Ribbons of cleared forest coming down from the high peaks, often ending in a flared shape, are avalanche and landslide tracks—places where snow and rock falling from above have flattened the trees in their path. Large clear patches, usually intersected by roads, are clearcuts. This is one of the major timber-producing areas on Earth, although the ancient forest is diminishing rapidly.

Off the coast you will see another kind of forest: underwater masses of kelp, a kind of seaweed. These dark patches just off the rocky shore are part of a rich marine ecosystem that includes wild salmon, seals, sea lions, orcas, baleen whales, and birds.

THE TAIGA

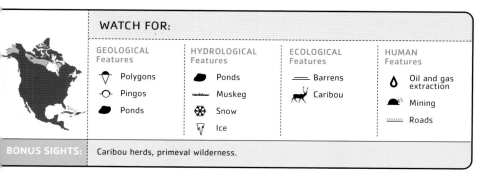

The permafrost patches of the taiga become larger and larger farther north, finally merging to cover the northern third of Canada. Barren stretches of tundra radiate outward as far as the eye can see. This is a remote region, almost completely unpopulated.

The treeline is the northernmost extent of continuous forest—the end of the taiga. To the north, you'll see the tundra, barrens that stretch for hundreds of miles to the Arctic Ocean. This landscape of lichens, moss, and struggling shrubs appears white and beige in the winter, green throughout the spring and summer, and red and yellow during the brief August autumn.

If you are flying over the barrenlands, keep an eye out for the caribou herds. You may be able to spot them during the summer as dark, antlike swarms on the otherwise light ground surface far below you. These are the world's largest groups of free-roaming large mammals: several herds of one million animals each migrate from the taiga each summer to calving grounds in the High Arctic.

During the profoundly cold eight-month-long winter, this land is frozen solid. The hardy locals find it far easier to travel on ice and snow than in the summer swamps, which swarm with billions of mosquitoes. Understandably, this is one of the least-populated parts of the globe.

Nunavut, Canada's newest territory, was created in 1999. It comprises two million square kilometers (770,000 square miles, larger than Alaska) of tundra and Arctic coastline that stretches from Hudson Bay to the North Pole. Yet this vast area supports just twenty-nine thousand residents in twenty-six communities, none of them accessible by road.

Most of the people here are indigenous—"Nunavut" means "our land" in the local Inuktitut language, and the establishment of the territory has allowed the traditional Inuit culture a measure of self-determination that had been lacking in the past.

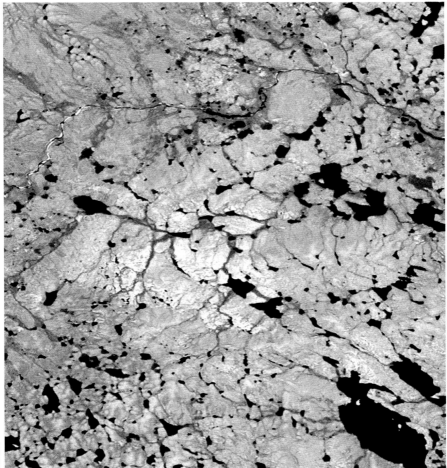

0 1km 1mi

BARRENS ➤ Permafrost underlies the tundra blanketing the profound wilderness of Nunavut above the Arctic Circle. The marshy barrens between waterways are covered by small, hardy plants and lichens. Watch for polygonal chunks of peatland formed by the action of underground networks of ice wedges beneath the seams. The entire landscape is frozen solid in winter.

the tundra
151

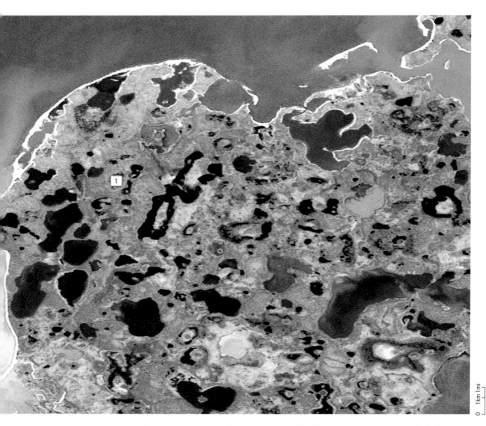

PINGOS ➤ The barrens and the Mackenzie Delta meet the Arctic Ocean near Tuktoyaktuk in the North West Territories. The ground here is frozen solid up to 700 m (2,300 feet) deep, and the permafrost continues out to sea, where the ocean floor is frozen. The circular features **1** in this cold, flat marsh—called pingos —are heaps of till that have been raised up to 100 m (330 feet) by the freezing and thawing cycle of old lakes beneath them.

0   1km 1mi

WATCH FOR:

GEOLOGICAL Features	HYDROLOGICAL Features	ECOLOGICAL Features	HUMAN Features
Islands	Glaciers	Not very many	Barely any
Mountains	Pack ice		
	Icebergs		
	The Arctic Ocean		

BONUS SIGHTS: Aurora borealis.

The Arctic, technically the part of the Northern Hemisphere that experiences at least one day of total darkness each winter and one day of midnight sun each summer, is the starkest of wildernesses.

The High Arctic, which includes northern Alaska, the northern islands of Canada (the largest archipelago on Earth), and Greenland (the world's largest island), begins as you leave the mainland and fly out over the Arctic Ocean. Here, you'll see pack ice—a jagged white crust covering the water and, in winter, creating a contiguous surface with the land. Farther north, the ice is permanent; this is the polar ice cap.

Sea ice is at its thickest in May, after building up for eight to ten months. Jammed hard against the coast, it blocks all sea passage and raises berms (walls of rubble) you might spot along flatter coastlines. Even when leads in the ice are open, they fill with drifting pack ice and icebergs (chunks of glaciers that have fallen into the sea—watch for taller, solitary blobs of white ice in the dark water).

The bleak surface belies the richness of the marine ecosystems below, however. These icy waters teem with fish, seals, and whales, the basis for local indigenous societies. Sixty thousand people live in Greenland, many still pursuing traditional resource-based livelihoods.

Chances are, by the time your plane gets to this part of North America, you've been flying for hours over land transformed again and again by glacial action. Well, now you're visiting the glaciers where they still live (see page 66 for more information about glaciers).

The ice cap covering Greenland (which, as Kallallit Nunaat, is an independent country within the Danish Commonwealth) contains

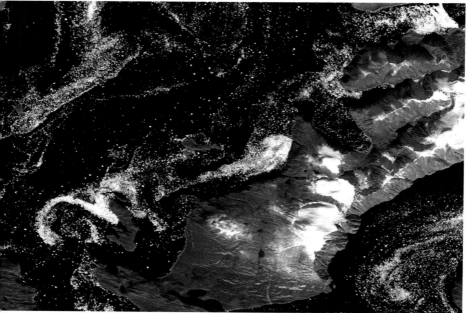

0 1km 1mi

PACK ICE ⊱ Arctic Ocean pack ice forms in the winter when it is cold enough for salt water to freeze. About 2 m (6.5 feet) thick, the ice—hunting ground for the polar bear—forms a continuous mass between the land and the perma- nent polar ice cap (which is 25 times thicker). The September ice here, at Delight Anchorage in Nunavut, is just beginning to form in eddies and swirls in the cold Arctic Ocean water.

one-tenth of the planet's fresh water and rises to 3,000 meters (10,000 ft.). Ice caps just like this once covered all of Canada. The deepest ice here is a magnificent record of global climatic history more than two million years old.

This is particularly important, because slight changes in global temperature strongly affect the Arctic. Atmospheric warming, caused by the release of greenhouse gases like carbon dioxide through human activity (including driving cars and flying jet planes), has resulted in glaciers here melting faster, pack ice retreating from the shore, and permafrost turning to larger and larger wetlands. Nobody knows what the global implications are of such changes to this vast region.

If you happen to be flying here during the polar night (winter), look out into the darkness and see if you can spot the aurora borealis (northern

THE ICE CAP ≻ These glaciers on Baffin Island are the remains of the ice sheet that once covered much of North America. Here, you will find the gamut of glacial landforms freshly minted. In this image, you can find fjords **1**, U-shaped valleys **2**, terminal **3** and lateral **4** moraines, arêtes **5**, and cirques **6**.

0 1 km 1 mi

lights). These breathtaking sheets of green and pink high in the sky are caused by subatomic particles that stream out of the Sun. Earth's magnetic field pushes them away from the atmosphere, except near the poles where the field goes into the planet. Between 80 and 640 kilometers (50 and 400 mi.) above Earth's surface, the high-energy particles strike gases in the atmosphere that release light as they are energized, much like in a fluorescent bulb.

Oxygen atoms emit green light and nitrogen atoms produce pink, although many other colors are also visible, sometimes including a deep red from high-altitude oxygen, 320 kilometers (200 mi.) from Earth, on the edge of space.

These mesmerizing phenomena figure prominently in the mythologies of people living throughout the Arctic. The Inuit—the people indigenous to most of Arctic North America—have studied these specters for generations and believe that they are the spirits of their ancestors.

the high arctic

THE SKY THE SKY THE SKY THE SKY THE SKY THE

THE SKY THE SKY THE
THE SKY THE **SKY** THE
SKY THE SKY THE S

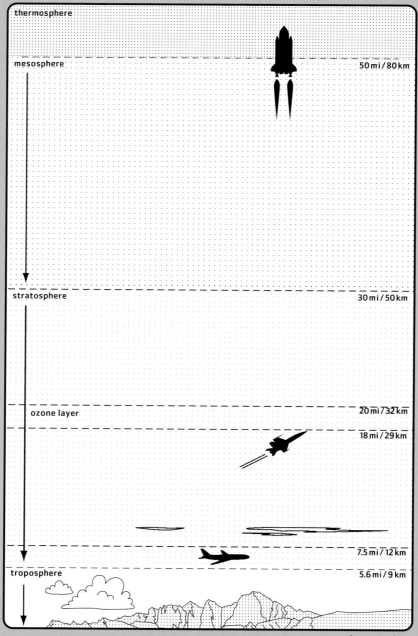

thermosphere

mesosphere 50 mi / 80 km

stratosphere 30 mi / 50 km

ozone layer 20 mi / 32 km

18 mi / 29 km

7.5 mi / 12 km

troposphere 5.6 mi / 9 km

the atmosphere

The atmosphere makes it possible for us to live on the surface of this planet—and to fly over it. Gravity holds this blanket of gases to Earth. As a result, the air is denser closer to the surface: Its bulk is within the first 18 miles (29 km)—about the highest a jet can fly. There is also a very, very thin atmospheric presence up to 50 miles (80 km)—the height at which NASA considers travelers to become astronauts.

At cruising altitude, your jet is flying in the thinner air between 30,000 and 40,000 feet (9 to 12 km). The atmosphere here imposes less drag on the aircraft while still supplying enough lift for efficient flight. Best of all, this altitude puts your flight path above most weather for a less-turbulent passage.

The atmosphere is divided into four main sections: the troposphere, to about 6 miles (10 km) up, the stratosphere, to about 30 miles (50 km), the mesosphere, to 50 miles (80 km), and the thermosphere thereafter for an indefinite and arbitrary distance.

The troposphere, where we live and where the weather we are familiar with takes place, is of the greatest interest to the air traveler. A transcontinental jet at cruising altitude—6 miles, or 32,000 feet (10 km)—is skirting the top of the troposphere in a zone called the tropopause and is about halfway to the ozone layer in the stratosphere. For comparison, space shuttles usually orbit Earth at about 250 miles (400 km) up.

Sooner or later, as you gaze out your airplane window, you'll find yourself looking down on an endless plain of fluffy clouds obscuring the world below. Take heart in the fact that at least you're enjoying the sun, while the poor souls on the ground are suffering through an overcast day—and take this opportunity to observe clouds from a new perspective.

Clouds are composed of liquid water and ice particles suspended in the atmosphere. Occurring in the troposphere and the lower reaches of the stratosphere, they are influenced by two primary factors: heat emanating from Earth's surface beneath them, and the jet-stream winds above them.

LIGHTNING

Cumulonimbus clouds often acquire internal electrical differentials as water droplets and ice crystals move within them, much as your body becomes charged when you shuffle across a carpet on a dry winter day. Lightning is the discharge of this energy between or within clouds or between clouds and the ground.

From the air, particularly at night, lightning is a spectacular sight as it illuminates the innards of huge thunderheads or spreads out across a cloud bank far below you. About 80 percent of lightning strikes within clouds, rather than between clouds and the ground, so from your high vantage point you'll see a lot of flashes you would otherwise miss.

Occasionally, lightning strikes an airplane, but not to worry: Because of Gauss's law, an effect whereby electrical charge distributed around a hollow metal object cancels itself out in the object's interior, people and electronics inside the plane are unaffected.

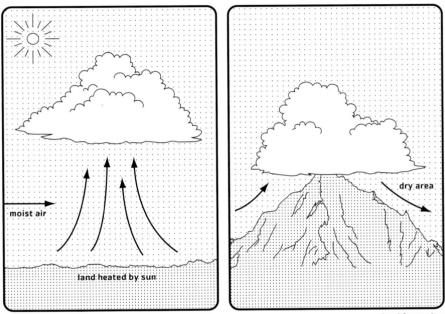

moist air

land heated by sun

dry area

cloud formation

A warm spot on the ground causes the air above it to rise. As air rises, it cools and thus loses some of its capacity to hold water. Water condenses out of the cooled air to form visible clouds. The type of cloud that develops varies according to local conditions, which in turn depend in part on surface features and in part on the movement of air masses.

Cumulus clouds, the classic thunderheads, arise from the strong uplift of moist air, often on humid summer days. Rising up to 11 miles (17 km), they are the clouds responsible for much of what we don't like about weather—rain, hail, snowstorms, and, for air travelers, turbulence. They do look magnificent, however: These giant plumes of bright white vapor and ice glow in the high-altitude sun like mountains of cotton candy.

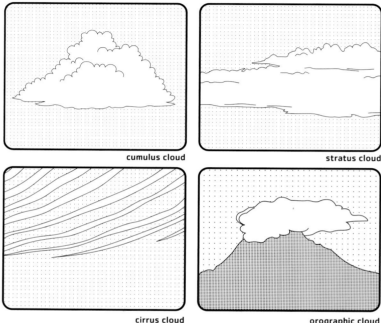

cumulus cloud

stratus cloud

cirrus cloud

orographic cloud

The life cycle of a cumulus cloud is about two hours. Young clouds have rounded tops, while more mature ones—those more likely to punish the people below with heavy weather—feature a flat-topped anvil shape in which water droplets have turned to ice.

Stratus clouds, arranged like sheets in the sky, are caused by inversions in which cooler air prevents warmer air beneath it from rising. Forming at the interface between these temperature zones, stratus clouds are responsible for the solid gray ceilings we so often encounter soon after takeoff. By the same token, these clouds become the floor of our vista once we break through into the brilliant blue skies above.

Cirrus clouds, the high, wispy strands you find at altitudes above 18,000 feet (5.5 km) or more, are the only clouds that are likely to be higher than your plane at cruising altitude on a long flight. If they look a little like blowing snow, it's no accident: They're composed of ice particles.

Orographic clouds, resulting from air being lifted by landforms such as mountains, can be any of the types already mentioned, as well as a few unique forms. One of the most striking of these is the lenticular cloud. Shaped like horizontal lenses, these are very smooth, rounded stratus clouds usually associated with mountains in otherwise clear skies and strong winds. Keep an eye out for them especially on clear winter days in western North America.

Because mountains can strip moisture from the air, downwind regions may experience a rain shadow. This is the reason the deserts in the western United States are so dry, for example: In California, the Coast Range and the Sierra Nevada wring the moisture from Pacific air masses before they move inland.

WHY IS THE SKY BLUE?

The color of the sky is so commonplace we often forget there is a reason for it: Molecules and atoms of the gases that make up the atmosphere (primarily nitrogen and oxygen) scatter blue light. Sunlight is made up of all the colors in the spectrum, and although the rest of them are able to pass straight through the atmosphere, allowing us to see the sun, blue light is scattered from every part of the sky, making it all appear blue.

Water vapor in the air also scatters light but does so indiscriminately: All colors are equally affected, making clouds look white.

Atmospheric blue scattering is also the reason the sun looks yellowish or orange. Because the blue part of the sun's light has been reduced by the time we see it, the sun appears warmer. In space, where scattering does not take place, the sun appears white and the sky black.

Weather is one effect of climate, a complex interaction between air masses, water, ice, land, and solar energy. Air masses generally move from west to east across North America, pushed along by high-altitude winds called the jet stream.

Blowing to more than 200 miles (320 km) per hour, the jet stream circles the planet 6 to 8 miles (10 to 13 km) above the surface. Because of these winds, a typical flight from Los Angeles to New York takes about an hour less than the reverse flight. Flights are routed to avoid headwinds and to take advantage of tailwinds in order to save fuel. These winds meander like a river, so your precise route across the continent can vary dramatically depending on where the jet stream happens to be that day.

When a cold air mass pushes into a warmer one, it shoulders the warm air upward, forming a cold front. Thunderstorms form in narrow squall lines hundreds of miles long along advancing cold fronts, followed by blankets of stratus clouds that form between the air masses.

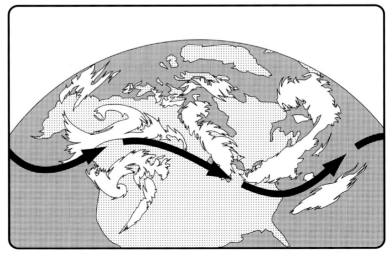

jet streams

GLORIES

As you gaze down at the clouds below you on a bright sunny day, you'll notice a unique atmospheric phenomenon directly opposite the sun, surrounding your plane's shadow. A glory, an aura of bright reddish and bluish bands radiating away from the shadow— or from the point where the shadow would be if it is not visible—is sunlight that has been diffracted and reflected back toward its source by water droplets in a cloud.

SMOG

Smog is that sickening brown haze seen above urban areas or other sources of pollution when there is an inversion—a layer of cool air sitting on top a mass of stable warm air. Such conditions are common in basins surrounded by higher ground, such as the Los Angeles region and the San Francisco Bay Area, but they can be found anywhere.

Pollutants, which can be from sources as diverse as fireplaces, factories, and forest fires but are overwhelmingly produced by motor vehicles, become trapped at this layer, unable to rise or dissipate. Under the action of the sun, gases and particles in the pollution chemically change and form the visible miasma that has, unfortunately, become a normal part of the view from airplane windows.

In a warm front, the same thing happens, but for the opposite reason: The advancing warm air mass climbs on top of the cold air as it moves forward. The first indication that you are approaching a warm front is a sky filled with cirrus clouds. Later, you'll see a blanket of stratus clouds. Closer to the front, you'll notice great masses of broad cumulus clouds, followed by thick stratus clouds.

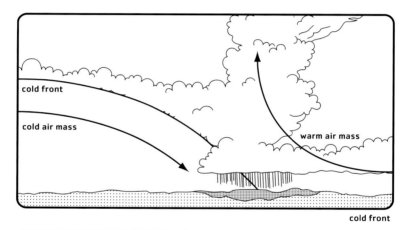

cold front

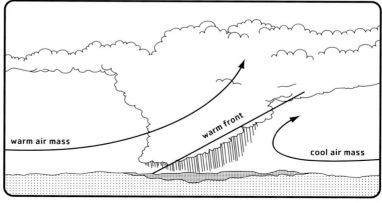

warm front

Three or four air masses are usually moving across North America at any one time, so chances are good you'll see a front on any flight longer than a couple of hours. If you have a newspaper handy, try to identify the front you are looking at in today's weather map and find out more about it.

CONTRAILS

Since you're flying along a jetway — an invisible highway in the sky — you're quite likely to see the contrails, or condensation trails, left behind by other planes. As the hot exhaust of their engines cools, water created when jet fuel is burned condenses into ice crystals, forming billowy white lines in the sky. With time, they are blown out into more natural-looking forms, particularly when the jet stream is strong.

Contrails are a visible manifestation of the air-transportation system. Astronauts have reported that these lines often radiate like starbursts from major destinations and are some of the most visible evidence of human activity on the planet.

You'll notice that contrails heading in directions different from your own will be at different altitudes. This vertical separation is a safety measure built into the system.

Trails that last a long time indicate humid air, while dry air makes them evaporate and disappear quickly. In extremely dry air, contrails may not form at all.

Where conditions are right, contrails can become cirrus clouds and can actually affect weather. The absence of commercial jet traffic for three days in September 2001, for example, resulted in clearer skies and greater ground-temperature variation across the United States.

AFTERWORD

If you're reading this, it must be cloudy, or nighttime. Or perhaps you're laid over between flights or your seatmate has insisted that you lower the shade so she can watch that infernal movie about talking dogs. For whatever reason, you're presently unable to gaze like a heavenly being across the unfolding continent.

But at least now you know what you're missing, and are probably looking forward to your next flight. There is simply nothing to compare with the view we get from a routine passenger flight. It's the special treat of an impossible view, available to millions every day. As with many things in life, very few of us take the time to really see what we are looking at, and in the process we cheat ourselves out of the wonder and majesty of our world.

Learning to read the landscape from the air is just one step anyone of us can take in coming to know our surroundings better and to appreciate deeply Earth's immensity and beauty. Seen in this light, the pedestrian experience of taking a flight becomes a new and very powerful way to appreciate our planet and our civilization.

Having read this book, I hope that you will never again just glance out the airplane window—or any window, for that matter—and idly wonder what it is you are looking at before going back to killing time with a spreadsheet or an airport novel. You won't see just a mountain; you'll see the colliding forces of tectonic plates, millions of years of erosion, and buzzing human activity on its flanks. You'll see more deeply, and in better focus than ever before.

I hope that you take this spirit with you wherever you go and however you get there, for the magnificence of existence is all around us; we just need to open ourselves to it to feel its full force. - *Gregory Dicum*

LIST OF FIGURES

list of figures

GLOSSARY

arête – a sharp mountain ridge formed between two glaciers

barrier island – a long, narrow, sandy island formed by ocean currents and wave action off the coast of the mainland

barrier reef – a long coral reef that parallels a coast

batholith – a body of granite that formed deep underground

bayou – a sluggish side channel in the Mississippi Delta

caldera – a crater left behind by a volcanic eruption

cinder cone – a dark or reddish pile of lava chunks left where a volcano has spewed them out

cirque – a rounded hollow in a mountainside where a glacier once sat

contrail – "condensation trails" of water vapor that form in the sky from a jet's exhaust

delta – a wide, marshy area of many channels where a river enters a larger body of water and drops its silt

drumlin (whaleback) hills – sloping hills left behind by glaciers; they often occur in groups, parallel to the direction of the glacier that formed them

esker – long, sinuous ridges that were once the beds of rivers that flowed under glaciers

estuary – an enclosed body of water where fresh river water mixes with salty seawater

exotic terranes – rock that originated far away from its present location

glory – a glowing aura on cloud tops around the shadow of an airplane

graben – a long depression between geological fault lines

hogback escarpment – a long, sharp ridge where a layer of rock emerges from the surrounding terrain

karst – a Swiss-cheese-like landscape where flat limestone has been eroded by water to form many sinkholes, caverns, and underground rivers

kettle pond – a round pond formed by a chunk of ice left over from a glacier

levee – a long mound of earth built near a river to contain floodwaters

meander – the snakelike progression of a river, or a winding bulge in a river's course

monadnock – a mass of hard rock that stands out from a flat plain that has eroded around it

moraine – a long ridge of sand and rock left behind by a glacier

muskeg – subarctic marsh often underlain by permafrost

oxbow lake – a long, curving lake left behind when a meander is cut off by changes in a river's course

permafrost – a layer of permanently frozen water and earth just under the ground surface that is responsible for many of the features in the Arctic and Subarctic

pingo – a round hill found in the High Arctic formed by the heaving action of underground ice

salt dome – an underground upwelling of semi-liquid salt that often accumulates oil and gas deposits

savanna – a wet grassland

sinkhole – the depression, often water filled, left behind when an underground cavern collapses

spillway – a broad channel where glacial meltwater once flowed

taiga – subarctic evergreen forest

tailing – waste rock left behind by a mining operation

watershed – the area that drains into a single body of water

LOG OF FLIGHTS

Date: .... Departure point: ....
Flight: .... Destination: ....
Sights: ....
....
....
....
....

Date: .... Departure point: ....
Flight: .... Destination: ....
Sights: ....
....
....
....
....

Date: .... Departure point: ....
Flight: .... Destination: ....
Sights: ....
....
....
....
....

Date: .... Departure point: ....
Flight: .... Destination: ....
Sights: ....
....
....
....

window seat